JOHN WESLEY

Holiness of Heart & Life

Charles Yrigoyen, Jr.

WITH STUDY GUIDE BY
Ruth A. Daugherty

ABINGDON PRESS
NASHVILLE

John Wesley: Holiness of Heart and Life

Copyright © 1996 Charles Yrigoyen, Jr.

The Study Guide for *John Wesley: Holiness of Heart and Life*
Copyright © 1996 Ruth A. Daugherty

This book is printed on acid-free paper.

Library of Congress Cataloging-in-Publication Data

Yrigoyen, Charles, 1937–
    John Wesley: holiness of heart and life/ Charles Yrigoyen, Jr.;
with study guide by Ruth A. Daugherty.
        p.   cm.
    Originally published: New York: Mission Education and Cultivation
Program Dept. for the Women's Division. General Board of Global
Ministries, United Methodist Church. c 1996.
    Includes bibliographical references.
    ISBN 0-687-05686-1 (pbk.)
    1. United Methodist Church (U.S.A.)—Study and teaching.
2. Methodist Church—United States—Study and teaching.   3. Wesley,
John. 1703–1791—Study and teaching.   I. Daugherty, Ruth A.
II. Title.
[BX8331.2.Y97   1999]
287'.6—dc21   98-43197
                                                                          CIP

02 03 04 05 06 07 08 — 10 9 8 7 6 5

MANUFACTURED IN THE UNITED STATES OF AMERICA

CONTENTS

Introduction... 5

CHAPTER 1
    John Wesley: A Person of Faith in an Age of Need 9
    Some Questions for Reflection and Discussion...................... 22

CHAPTER 2
    "Plain Truth": Main Themes in John Wesley's Theology 23
    Some Questions for Reflection and Discussion...................... 39

CHAPTER 3
    "Works of Piety": Spiritual Formation in the Wesleyan Tradition 40
    Some Questions for Reflection and Discussion...................... 56

CHAPTER 4
    "Works of Mercy": The Practice of the Holy Life and the
        Transformation of Society 57
    Some Questions for Reflection and Discussion...................... 73

CHAPTER 5
    Wesley's People in North America........................... 74
    Some Questions for Reflection and Discussion...................... 92

CHAPTER 6
    Renewal in the Wesleyan Tradition 93
    Some Questions for Reflection and Discussion...................... 105

Glossary... 106

Study Guide 111

Selected Bibliography...................................... 155

For
Deb and Michael
Chuck, Paula, Darin, and Hunter

INTRODUCTION

The United Methodist Church is a union of two main traditions, Methodism and the Evangelical United Brethren. Each of these traditions brought significant histories, ministries, and achievements to their union in 1968. Although the Evangelical United Brethren traced their origins to a different set of circumstances, nevertheless they were, like their Methodist sisters and brothers, much influenced by John Wesley's views of the Christian faith and the mission of the church long before the union took place.

The purpose of this book is to examine the historic roots of United Methodism in the life, thought, and ministry of John Wesley (1703–1791), the founder of Methodism. It is the basic assumption of this book that Wesley can teach us much about who we are, from whence we have come, and what God calls us to do as we celebrate God's grace and witness for Jesus Christ. As we consider Wesley's ideas and his practice of Christian faith and mission, we hope to discover a vision for the renewal of our personal lives and the life of our church.

Since the focus of the book is Wesley and the origins and development of the Methodist side of our denominational history, the term "Methodist" appears frequently instead of "United Methodist" in order to maintain historical perspective and accuracy. Perhaps a future book will highlight the important personalities, events, and contributions of the Evangelical United Brethren tradition that have also made United Methodism what it is. We give thanks for our rich United Methodist heritage.

Since there is considerable debate across United Methodism about the nature of the faith and the mission of the church, this is an appropriate time to reconsider John Wesley's understanding of the Christian faith and life. Some claim that our church must be more actively engaged in evangelism—calling people to repentance and announcing God's offer of forgiveness and new life in Christ—and helping people to realize deeper spiritual life. That is the mission of the church, they say. Others hold that we must be more aggressively involved in changing social conditions—feeding the hungry, housing the homeless, healing the sick, fighting injustice, and serving the poor and oppressed. That is our mission, they contend.

Wesley's understanding of mission includes both! It is thoroughly evangelistic and aims at spiritual maturity. It is just as thoroughly devoted to changing the social conditions in which we live. "Works of piety" and "works of mercy," two wonderful Wesleyan expressions, remind us of his wholistic approach to mission.

This is also a time in which there is much contention about doctrine and theology in United Methodism, some of which has been carried on antagonistically. It has been suggested that we re-examine Wesley's attitude toward doctrine and theology. What can we learn from him? How did he formulate his understanding of the Christian faith, and how did he live it out in his own life? What were the central points in his theology? According to Wesley, how should we act toward others whose theological views differ from ours? In his Letter to a Roman Catholic (1749) Wesley wrote, "If we cannot as yet think alike in all things, at least we may love alike." What lesson is there for us in these words?

It may be useful to trace the direction in which we will be moving in this book. In Chapter 1 we will give a brief account of John Wesley's life and the context in which it was lived. Chapter 2 outlines the sources and main themes of Wesley's understanding of the Christian faith and life, the culmination of which is holiness of heart and life. Chapter 3 describes the disciplines that the Christian employs and by which God provides the grace necessary for faith to grow and mature. Chapter 4 discusses the mission of the Christian person and community in doing good to others. Chapter 5 offers a brief sketch of the Methodists in North America and shows how Wesley's theology (which we have considered in Chapter 2), his views on spiritual formation (considered in Chapter 3), and his understanding of mission (treated in Chapter 4) were adapted to the American scene. Chapter 6 deals with the same three themes treated in Chapters 2, 3, and 4: theology, spiritual formation, and mission in the Wesleyan tradition in light of our present calling.

Throughout the book there are many quotes from John Wesley's sermons and other writings. Many of them are identified with their source in Wesley's writings, but not every quote or idea from Wesley is so noted. In some quotes Wesley's language has been changed to make it more inclusive. In others, however, changing the language seemed to disrupt the forcefulness of his prose, rhythm, and style, so it has not been altered. It is hoped that this book will prompt those who read it to read more about John Wesley and, even more fittingly, to read more of Wesley's own writings.

A few hymns of Charles Wesley are cited in the text because both brothers understood that Charles's hymns conveyed the heart of the Wesleyan message in a way that all Methodists could know and voice through their singing. Readers are also encouraged to use the United Methodist Book of Discipline, Book of Resolutions, Book of Worship, and Hymnal. These resources contain information and insights about our Wesleyan identity and mission to strengthen our worship, fellowship, and ministry together.

Terms marked with an asterisk (*) are more fully explained in the Glossary. Quotes from the Bible are from the New Revised Standard Version except within quotes from Wesley, who used the English Scriptures available at the time. These were the Authorized or King James Version of the Bible and the Psalms and other readings included in *The Book of Common Prayer** from an earlier translation. You will find several Scripture references in parentheses. Some of these quotes and references come from Wesley's writings, but many of them have been added by this author to illustrate further the relationship of Wesley's views to biblical ideas.

Several people have read the manuscript for this book and made helpful suggestions to improve it. I am deeply grateful to Kenneth E. Rowe, a colleague at the Archives and History Center of The United Methodist Church, and to my wife Jean for their invaluable comments. I also wish to thank the Women's Division of the General Board of Global Ministries who used an earlier version of the book as a mission study text. Inadequacies that remain are the sole responsibility of the author.

1

CHAPTER

JOHN WESLEY

A Person of Faith in an Age of Need

On his 85th birthday, John Wesley, the founder of Methodism, paused to reflect on his life and ministry. He wrote in his journal for June 28, 1788 (old calendar):

> It is true I am not so agile as I was in times past. I do not run or walk so fast as I did; my sight is a little decayed; my left eye is grown dim, and hardly serves me to read; I have daily some pain in the ball of my right eye, as also in my right temple . . . and in my right shoulder and arm, which I impute partly to a strain, and partly to the rheumatism. I find likewise some decay in my memory in regard to names and things lately passed, but not at all with regard to what I have read or heard twenty, forty, or sixty years ago; neither do I find any decay in my hearing, smell, taste, or appetite (though I want but a third . . . of the food I did once); nor do I feel any such thing as weariness, either in traveling or preaching; and I am not conscious of any decay in writing sermons, which I do as readily, and, I believe, as correctly, as ever.
>
> *(Journal, June 28, 1788)*

During the next week, the elderly Wesley kept the same energetic pace that had marked his ministry for more than fifty years. He preached sixteen times in twelve different towns. He attributed his extraordinary spiritual keenness and physical strength to God's power at work in his life, the vital prayers and support of his brothers and sisters in the faith, and his disciplined life.

Who was this man whose faith and ministry inspired thousands of people in his time, who decisively changed religion and society in the eighteenth century and after, and who is considered the spiritual parent of a worldwide community of churches with approximately thirty million members in 96 countries?

John Wesley was born June 17, 1703 (new calendar), in the small town of Epworth in Lincolnshire in northeastern England. His life encompassed almost the entire eighteenth century, an era in which major changes were occurring, especially in England and North America. It is difficult to give a brief description of eighteenth-century English life. Nevertheless, we must try to understand it in order to provide the historical context for the life and ministry of John Wesley. Eighteenth-century England was politically more stable than during the previous century, when there was a bloody civil war. Political strife continued between the two major parties, the conservative Tories and the reformist Whigs. England's military and economic strength were on the ascendant. The population of England in the early eighteenth century numbered about five million; by the end of the century it had increased to more than eight million. About 10 percent of the populace lived in London, a great many in severe poverty. No other English city came close to London in size; although by the century's end the number of towns and cities and their population were growing, especially industrial centers like Manchester, Birmingham, and Leeds.

Life in the cities and larger towns was precarious, especially for the numerous poor. Regular employment was uncertain. Housing was often inadequate and unaffordable. The poorer sections of the cities were usually overcrowded, ramshackle slums of filth and squalor. Sanitation was primitive. Merchants and families discarded their refuse in the streets and rivers, where it decayed with a horrible stench. Pure drinking water was scarce. Nourishing food was often costly and in short supply. Disease was rampant, especially in the homes of the poor. Life was insecure. Alcohol, violence, prostitution, and gambling were popular means to escape feelings of desperation and hopelessness.

Artisans, skilled laborers, and apprentices constituted a slowly growing middle class, whose situation was less grave. Still, fourteen-hour workdays were routine and wages low. A working man's income was sometimes supplemented by a small additional income from the employment of his wife and children. Children as young as four or five were employed as chimney sweeps or in mines and factories.

The wealthy were relatively few in number but extremely powerful. Some had inherited immense fortunes. Others had amassed money and property through exploitive business opportunities and shrewd dealing. The lives of landowners, aristocrats, and rich merchants were marked by extravagance, comfort, and ease, in stark contrast to the futile situation of the poor. During the eighteenth century the English population became more polarized along economic lines.

Most English people lived in rural areas and small towns. They farmed the land, raised cattle and sheep, fished the rivers and seas, worked the mines and quarries, and provided the services that every village and town needed to survive such as milling, baking, tailoring, shoeing horses, and repairing wagons. Life was not quite as precarious for many of these folks as for the poor in the cities, but the circumstances of the rural middle and working classes were not easy either. Proprietors of small businesses eked out their livings as best they could. Farm laborers were usually tenants who had to pay rent regardless of how poor the harvest might be. It was extremely difficult for the poor to break the bonds of their poverty or for anyone new to move into the ranks of the wealthy.

As the eighteenth century unfolded, England underwent major economic and social changes. New technologies in farming and manufacturing led to increased production. Basic industries such as textiles and iron smelting made significant improvements. The development of steam power proved important for industrial growth. Turnpikes and canals improved the transport of raw materials and manufactured goods. England was in the early stages of the Industrial Revolution.

The great majority of the population claimed at least nominal adherence to the Church of England, the realm's Established or official state church. There were also smaller numbers of Roman Catholics and nonconforming or dissenting churches such as the Presbyterians, Congregationalists, Baptists, and Quakers. The Established Church was intricately connected to the political world. Parish boundaries had been drawn up centuries before, so some newer towns and villages did not even have parish churches or clergy. Members of other faiths could not vote or sit in Parliament, partly in reaction to the previous century's strife against both Catholics and Puritans. The Established Church saw its mission as maintaining the status quo and urging people to accept their place in God's scheme of things. Spiritual and moral guidance was usually offered in that direction. Despite the good intentions and sincere efforts of many clergy and laity, the church did little to improve the lot of the poor. It was in this England that John Wesley was born and his ministry developed.

John Wesley was one of nineteen children born to Samuel Wesley and his wife, Susanna Annesley. Both parents were the children of dissenting or Puritan clergy and understood "church" as more than the Established Church. Samuel Wesley, himself the son and grandson of clergy, converted to the Church of England while at Oxford and became a priest who served the parish of Epworth in the watery flats of Lincolnshire for nearly forty years. He was a strict, conscientious parish priest who had a genuine love for scholarship and poetry. While not a great scholar or poet himself, he published a commentary on the Book of Job. Most of his work was lost in a household fire; one of his surviving hymns, "Behold the Savior of Mankind," is found in *The United Methodist Hymnal* (293).

At least two major problems plagued Samuel during his years at Epworth. First, he did not manage money well and on one occasion landed in debtors' prison in Lincoln. Second, some of the Epworth parishioners resented his strictness and showed their contempt by injuring his animals; destroying his crops; and, it was suspected, even setting fire to the rectory that burned to the ground in 1709. Fortunately, none of the family was hurt in the blaze. John, a lad of five, was the last child to be rescued from the burning home.

Susanna Annesley Wesley was an unusual person and is considered by many to be the stronger of the two parents. She was a committed Christian and parson's wife. She managed the household, bore and raised the children, and gave them their earliest education. She read widely, especially religious and theological literature, and conducted prayer meetings in the rectory in her husband's absence. Susanna and Samuel did not always agree on matters of religion and politics, which sometimes created serious tension in the rectory. The family's poverty and the continual births and deaths of children were other sources of stress.

Of the nineteen children, only ten survived into adulthood, including John. The oldest child, Samuel, Jr., became a priest in the Church of England. The seven sisters, Emilia, Susanna, Mary, Mehetabel, Anne, Martha, and Kezia, had very difficult lives. Their stories are told in Frederick E. Maser's book *The Story of John Wesley's Sisters, or Seven Sisters in Search of Love*. Several times John expressed his disappointment that his sisters were not more active in the Methodist movement, but they were coping with poverty and family problems. John's younger brother, Charles, became his closest friend and ally in his ministry. Like his father and both older brothers, Charles was ordained into the priesthood of the Church of England. He became committed to evangelical religion and used his considerable poetic talents to become the great hymn writer of Methodism. He wrote more than six thousand hymns, some of which are found in the hymnals of many different denominations. Among the best known are "Hark, the Herald Angels Sing," "O For a Thousand Tongues to Sing," and "Love Divine, All Loves Excelling."

Life in the Epworth rectory left a lasting impression on John Wesley. There he learned to love the Bible and the prayerbook of the Church of England. Under the influence of his parents he acquired a respect for scholarship, the teachings of the church, the disciplines of the Christian life, and missions. He valued these for the rest of his life and fondly recalled many of his Epworth experiences to the end of his ministry.

John's formal education was the best available at the time. In 1714, he was sent to Charterhouse, an exclusive school that prepared him to enter Oxford University. He matriculated at Christ Church College, Oxford, in 1720. When he graduated in 1724, Wesley had read widely in classical and modern literature, had studied theology, history, and science, and had become proficient in reading the New Testament in the original Greek.

As his Oxford graduation approached, he showed more concern for religious matters with the encouragement of his parents. It was not surprising, therefore, that he followed his father and brother into the priesthood of the Church of England.

John continued to live in Oxford, being honored with election to a fellowship at Lincoln College in March 1726. Unless requested to do so, fellows were not obliged to reside or perform duties at the college. Therefore, Wesley was free to spend considerable time away from Oxford helping his father with parish duties, which he did full time from 1727 through late 1729. Although John was ordained to the priesthood at Oxford in July 1728, apparently he had become convinced that the life of a parish priest was not for him.

In September 1729, Wesley was requested by the Lincoln College administration to perform teaching duties. In the meantime, his brother Charles had become a student at Christ Church and was a member of a small group of Oxford students who met regularly for the purpose of spiritual growth. John was invited to join them and soon became their unofficial leader. Under his direction they practiced the disciplines of prayer, Bible study, fasting, receiving Holy Communion, and engaging in social work, especially visiting the Oxford prisons and caring for the poor. Other students scornfully referred to this little society as "the Sacramentarians," "Bible moths," "the Holy Club," and "the Methodists."* Eventually, the latter name became the accepted title for Wesley's followers.

During these years Wesley was impressed with the pattern of life he believed existed among the earliest Christians and became convinced that he should imitate it. Some of his closest friends dubbed him "Primitive Christianity" even before he took up his role as leader of the Oxford "Methodists." Although the disciplined life of the small circle of Oxford students closely followed the example of the early Christians, Wesley became persuaded that God demanded more of him. After his father's death in 1735, he and Charles enlisted as missionaries of the Society for the Propagation of the Gospel, the missionary agency of the Church of England. This, he believed, imitated the early Christians' commitment to self-denial and complete surrender to God.

In the fall of 1735, both Wesley brothers set sail for the new colony of Georgia, in America. After a harrowing two-month voyage, they landed on February 6, 1736. John Wesley had at least three goals in mind: to minister to the English-speaking colonists in Georgia, to convert Native Americans to Christianity, and to gain an assurance of his own that God loved him.

The mission to Georgia lasted less than two years and was hardly a success. Although Wesley labored faithfully and energetically, he found many of his parishioners either indifferent or resistant to his ministry. Contacts with Native Americans were infrequent and unproductive. Furthermore, he had a disastrous romance with one of his parishioners, Sophy Hopkey, which led to his fleeing the colony under indictment by its Grand Jury. In December 1737, John Wesley boarded a ship and headed back to England; Charles had returned earlier.

Yet the American experience was not without a positive note. On his way to Georgia, during his stay in the colony and on his return to England, Wesley had become acquainted with Moravians, German pietists* who were under the spiritual leadership of Count Nicholas Ludwig von Zinzendorf. The Moravians taught a simple personal faith within an intimate disciplined fellowship. Wesley found them comforting Christian companions, even though he envied their confident trust and experience of God's presence.

The circumstances of the Georgia mission and his contact with the Moravians made Christianity a more personal question for Wesley. Confidence in his determination and ability to live a holy life pleasing to God was seriously shaken. The way was prepared for another stage in his understanding, experience, and practice of the Christian faith. Wesley remained spiritually distressed for several months after his return to England. He was searching for a faith that completely trusted God. He pondered returning to Oxford but was uncertain that it was the right course. He contemplated not preaching any longer, but conversations with his Moravian friend Peter Bohler convinced him that he should preach the kind of faith for which he was searching until he possessed it himself.

On the evening of May 24, 1738, while attending a prayer meeting on Aldersgate Street in London, something occurred that changed Wesley and the future course of his ministry. He described it in his journal:

> In the evening I went very unwillingly to a society in Aldersgate Street, where one was reading Luther's Preface to the Epistle to the Romans. About a quarter before nine, while he was describing the change which God works in the heart through faith in Christ, I felt my heart strangely warmed. I felt I did trust in Christ, Christ alone for salvation, and an assurance was given me, that he had taken away my sins, even mine and saved me from the law of sin and death.   *(Journal, May 24, 1738)*

Charles Wesley had had a similar experience just three days before. Aldersgate was an important step in John's religious experience and transformed his understanding and practice of the gospel. It did not insulate him from the problems with which all Christians must cope, such as temptation, doubt, and despair. Later he occasionally complained that he did not experience the peace, joy, and love that he believed ought to characterize the life of a believer. However, Aldersgate did convince him that the holiness he sought does not begin with human striving but by trusting the pardoning and empowering grace of God in Christ.

Anxious to build on the insights and experience of May 24, Wesley decided to visit the headquarters of his Moravian friends at Herrnhut in Germany. For several days he observed the style of their community life and conversed with their leader Zinzendorf. He was especially impressed with the intimacy and mutual care demonstrated among the Moravians. Several months after his visit to Herrnhut, however, he complained that the Moravians waited too passively for God's saving grace to work in their lives. He felt they were mistaken in not actively employing the means of grace that God supplied, such as prayer, Bible study, and the Lord's Supper, to hasten their conversion.

Upon his return to England in the fall of 1738, Wesley became engrossed in religious activity. Reading, studying, praying, visiting prisoners, celebrating Holy Communion, and preaching the evangelical message of God's unmerited love in Christ occupied his time. As he preached from place to place with no settled parish of his own, he observed that people were being changed by God through his declaration of the gospel. His work as an itinerant preacher had begun. It was to take an important turn in April 1739 when, persuaded by his friend George Whitefield, he moved outside church buildings and began to preach in the open air in Bristol. He reflected on this step in his journal:

> At four in the afternoon I submitted to "be more vile," and proclaimed in the highways the glad tidings of salvation, speaking from a little eminence in a ground adjoining to the city to about three thousand people. The Scripture on which I spoke was this (is it possible anyone should be ignorant that it is fulfilled in every true minister of Christ?): "The Spirit of the Lord is upon me, because he hath anointed me to preach the Gospel to the poor. He has sent me to heal the brokenhearted, to preach deliverance to the captives and recovery of sight to the blind, to set at liberty them that are bruised, to proclaim the acceptable year of the Lord." *(Journal, April 2, 1739)*

Wesley began to proclaim the evangelical message of God's forgiving grace in Christ wherever a group of listeners could be gathered.

16

To churches, homes, marketplaces, the entrances to mines, and other sites he took the message of the gospel, traveling by horse or carriage. By some estimates he logged as many as 250,000 miles during the course of his itinerancy. He visited not only England's cities, towns, and farms but also regularly journeyed to Wales, Scotland, and Ireland.

Unlike George Whitefield, whose preaching moved thousands to repentance and faith but who provided no separate structure for their nurture, Wesley decided that it was necessary to organize the people converted under his ministry. They were from every class and economic group. A few were wealthy. Some came from the ranks of shopkeepers. Most were members of the working class or poor. Many testified to the ways in which God's grace experienced through Methodist preaching and prayer had lifted them from drunkenness, family violence, prostitution, crime, and desperation to a new life of love, hope, and joy.

Wesley sought to devise a way for these people to grow in grace and be encouraged to attain holiness. He drew on the Anglican religious societies of his day, the Moravian groups in which he had participated, and the Oxford Holy Club as models for a structure for his Methodist people. Organized into society* groups, they could meet weekly for fellowship, preaching, prayer, and hymn-singing. They would have to meet at a time different from the local Church of England parish services, however, since Wesley wanted his people to attend faithfully the worship in their parishes where they would receive Holy Communion and have their children baptized.

Methodism, after all, was not intended to be a new church but a renewal movement within the Church of England. So Methodist societies, large and small, were formed wherever there were sufficient members to establish them. Among the earliest were those in London and Bristol. Anyone who desired to "flee from the wrath to come" and who intended to lead a holy life was welcomed into their fellowship. Members agreed to follow three General Rules: avoid evil, do good, and employ the means of grace God gives for spiritual growth. Disciplined Christian life was highly prized in the early Methodist movement.

In due course, and almost by accident, Wesley discovered a way the societies could be divided into smaller groups or "classes"* that would provide for even more intimate spiritual support and nurture. These classes were composed of about a dozen persons who met once a week with a class leader for spiritual conversation and guidance. Members spoke about their temptations, confessed their faults, shared their concerns, testified to the working of God in their lives, and exhorted and prayed for one another to be more faithful. Classes were designed to be centers of Christian love for the Methodist community. Every Methodist was expected to attend class meetings, which also issued and renewed the tickets required for admission to some other Methodist gatherings. For the more spiritually advanced, Wesley devised smaller groups or "bands,"* but these did not have the longevity of the societies and classes. In the earlier days of the movement, Wesley knew the members of his societies, bands, and classes by name.

Methodism flourished under the direction of class and band leaders, persons of spiritual strength and insight. Most of them were women. Among them were Sarah Crosby, Dorothy Downes, and Grace Murray, exemplary Christians whose witness persuaded many to accept God's grace and begin a new life.

As Methodism grew, Wesley adopted lay preachers as helpers and assistants. Some of them were full-time itinerants who served groups of societies called circuits. Others ministered in their spare time in the local area where they lived.

While Wesley had some doubts about the propriety of allowing women to preach, he recognized the deep Christian commitment and talents of Sarah Crosby, Mary Bosanquet, Hannah Harrison, Eliza Bennis, and others. In effect, these women were engaged in preaching; and many people experienced conversion as a result of their testimony and proclamation of the gospel. Wesley recognized their effectiveness and gave his blessing to their labors. In 1787, despite the objections of some of the male preachers, he officially authorized Sarah Mallet to preach, as long as she proclaimed the doctrines and adhered to disciplines that all Methodist preachers were expected to accept.

Although Wesley believed that opposition to women's preaching receded during the last years of his life, sentiment against them was rekindled after his death in 1791. The 1803 Conference in Manchester decided that women should not be permitted to preach because (1) a "vast majority" of the Methodist people opposed it; and (2) there were sufficient men to supply all the preaching places. It was conceded that if any woman had "an extraordinary call from God to speak in public . . . she should, in general, address her own sex and those only." Furthermore, any woman who desired to preach was required to obtain official permission from the local superintendent-preacher before doing so *(Minutes of the Methodist Conferences,* 1803). The role of women during the earlier period of the Methodist movement is effectively told by Paul W. Chilcote in *She Offered Them Christ: The Legacy of Women Preachers in Early Methodism* (Abingdon Press, 1993). In 1744, Wesley began to meet with his preachers annually, which marked the origin of the annual conference. At these annual gatherings there were discussions about theology and the mission of Methodism, and the preachers were appointed to their locations for the ensuing year.

As early as 1739, Wesley's concern for places for his societies to meet led him to construct chapels. The first was located in Bristol and became known as the New Room. It was not only a place for worship and preaching but also contained living quarters for Wesley when he visited the city. The New Room is presently maintained by British Methodism and is open to visitors. In 1739, Wesley also purchased and remodeled an old cannon factory in London that was known as the Foundry. It contained a chapel, lodgings for Wesley, and facilities for publishing and served as a center for various social ministries. Other Methodist chapels were constructed in many towns and villages and became gathering places for Methodist worship and ministry.

Wesley was not content simply to preach and to provide meeting places for his people. His vision of mission and ministry was much broader: he founded dispensaries for the sick, homes for orphans, and schools for the poor. He led the Methodists in personal visitation and care of the imprisoned and impoverished. He published books, pamphlets, and tracts to enhance the spiritual life and improve the physical health of any who wished to read them. In a later chapter we will explore more deeply his conviction that the gospel of Christ was meant for the whole person and for the whole human race, regardless of social standing.

Wesley and his people were not free from controversy and persecution. Although many of the Anglican* clergy and laity were friendly to Methodism's leader and followers, others created serious problems for them, especially in the early years of the movement. Some opposed Wesley's irregular preaching in the open air. Others disliked his plain speaking about sin and his proclamation of an evangelical experience, which they considered dangerously emotional. Still others resented his use of lay preachers and his disregard of parish boundaries as he itinerated from place to place.

Some men accused Wesley of undermining family values because, they complained, their women spent too much time at Methodist chapels and doing Methodist works such as visiting the sick. He was suspected of creating a schism in the Church of England. Extremists alleged that he was a Roman Catholic in disguise who sought to undermine both church and state. Although some accurate information circulated about Wesley and Methodists, many people formed opinions about them based on rumor and misinformation.

Methodists were attacked in cartoons and satires. Much more serious were well-documented incidents of mob violence against Wesley, his preachers, and people. Sometimes Wesley's followers feared for their lives. Some of the worst riots occurred at Wednesbury, near Birmingham, in 1743–44. Wesley collected sworn statements from a number of Wednesbury Methodists describing how mobs shattered the windows of their homes, pelted them with dirt and stones, destroyed their furniture, beat them with clubs, broke into their shops, smashed roof tiles, stole their belongings, and threatened to kill them. Only because they were Methodists! The local magistrates refused to come to their aid (*Modern Christianity: Exemplified at Wednesbury*, 1745). Both John and Charles Wesley described in their journals the ferocity of mobs in several towns and villages where people were intent on injuring them and on some occasions succeeded.

As the years progressed, violent persecution came to an end; but the leader and his followers continued to engage in theological disputes on such issues as predestination (i.e., whether human beings have free will to respond to the forgiveness and reconciliation that God offers), the relationship between faith and reason, the possibility of achieving perfection in this life, the Methodist emphasis on religious experience, and whether the Methodists should leave the Church of England. Wesley was never one to back away from theological controversy about issues he felt were central to faith.

Other issues clouded Wesley's life. One of them had to do with romantic relationships. We have already mentioned the disastrous ending of his friendship with Sophy Hopkey, one of his parishioners in Georgia. In 1748, he fell in love with Grace Murray, a Methodist widow thirteen years younger than he. They intended to marry; but through the intervention of Charles Wesley, Grace married another Methodist preacher. John despaired over this situation and was extremely angry with his brother's interference. The incident almost caused an irreparable break in their relationship.

John finally married in February, 1751, but not very successfully. He was far from a good husband. He and his wife, a widow named Mary (Molly) Vazeille, encountered major problems within a few years of their marriage. He was inattentive to her needs, devoting his time and energy to Methodist work. Molly was discouraged by his continual absence and jealous of his closeness to many of the women in the Methodist movement. The couple separated several times, beginning in 1757. When his wife died in October, 1781, Wesley was out of town and did not attend her funeral.

A second problem was the accusation leveled against Wesley that he was dictatorial in his management of the Methodist movement. He did govern Methodism with a determination that it was and would remain consistent with his dreams and ideals for it. After all, he reasoned, he was its parent. He had few reservations about imposing his will at every place where a key decision was to be made. The movement was not a democracy, he stated; and anyone who did not like the way it was run was free to leave. Some of his people, including a few of his preachers, resented his domineering attitude. The vast majority of Methodists, however, held him in the highest regard. By the end of his life he had also gained the respect of a large segment of the British population.

At the end of February, 1791, a few months short of his 88th birthday, Wesley became seriously ill. Friends and family gathered around his bed suspecting that he would not survive. During his last night he tried to sing Isaac Watt's hymn, "I'll praise my Maker while I've breath, And when my voice is lost in death, Praise shall employ my nobler powers." He was too weak to say more than, "I'll praise . . . I'll praise." As his life continued to ebb, he struggled to say what are believed to be his last words, "The best of all is, God is with us." On the morning of March 2, 1791, he died. There was not much to leave in his will. Over the years he had given away almost all his money to those in need. His will did provide for paying the six poor men who carried his coffin to its grave behind the Methodist chapel on City Road in London.

John Wesley was not without faults and inconsistencies. One commentator has described him as "a cluster of paradoxes," another as "the elusive Mr Wesley." Sometimes it appears that the Methodist movement succeeded because of him; often it seems to have succeeded in spite of him. He was, however, completely dedicated to bringing the gospel of Christ to bear on the lives of everyone he met, to meeting the needs of his age, and to spreading holiness across the land.

We will see more of that in the pages that follow. First, however, we must try to understand the basis on which Wesley's ministry was founded. What did he consider to be central to the Christian faith and its practice?

Some Questions for Reflection and Discussion

1. What did you know about John Wesley before reading this chapter? What new insights about Wesley have you gained as a result of studying the chapter?

2. Wesley was committed to relating the Christian faith to the needs of his age. What are the principal needs of our time? How do we decide how our faith is related to the needs we observe?

3. There were times, even late in his life, when Wesley's self-examination led him to say that he was not a Christian. Have you ever felt that way? If so, why? What have you found to be comforting and reassuring when you have had such feelings?

4. Although he was sometimes reluctant, Wesley often found that it was necessary to understand and to do things in new and different ways. For example, he preached in the open air; organized his people into societies, bands, and classes; and encouraged women to be leaders in the Methodist movement. What was his motivation for adopting different, even radical, approaches to ministry? What can we learn from him?

2

"PLAIN TRUTH"

Main Themes in John Wesley's Theology

Many people, especially outside Methodist circles, believe that John Wesley was not much of a theologian. They believe that his understanding of the Christian faith was entirely based on personal religious experience, without much attention to its content or to the sources from which it was drawn. This view is mistaken: Wesley was a theologian. The purpose of this chapter is threefold. First, it briefly describes the places where Wesley's theology may be found. Second, it examines the sources from which he drew his understanding of the Christian faith and life. Finally, it sets forth the main theological themes that Wesley identified as critical to Christianity.

Where to Find Wesley's Theology

John Wesley effectively used the printing press, the best means available to him other than his preaching, to make known his views on salvation, the Christian life, and the transformation of society. He was a prodigious writer, editor, and publisher. One edition of his collected writings includes thirty-five large volumes. Sometimes his printed work came from his own pen. At other times he freely borrowed, edited, and published the work of others. His aim was always to put into the hands of his Methodist followers and preachers what he considered "plain truth for plain people," literature that would enhance their experience of God's grace, deepen their knowledge of the faith, and at the same time challenge them to live a more holy life.

Reading Wesley's writings is both interesting and inspirational, although the reader must be prepared to deal with the peculiarities of the eighteenth-century language and style in which they were composed. It is also helpful to have some knowledge of what was happening in church and society at the time to appreciate more fully the main thrust of his positions and views on many matters.

The main themes of Wesley's theology are laced through his letters, diaries, and journal; his sermons and commentaries on the Bible; his books and pamphlets; and the collections of hymns that he and his brother Charles produced. Together these reveal a rich collection of insights about Christianity, Wesley's personal life and activities, and the origin and development of the early Methodist movement and its mission.

The most important of Wesley's theological writings are his sermons, his *Explanatory Notes Upon the New Testament*, and the hymnbooks he published. A brief comment about each of these is necessary.

Wesley believed that one of the best ways to provide sound Christian teaching for his people was to print some of his sermons. Over the course of his ministry he published 132 sermons written between 1730 and 1791, a small selection of the thousands that he preached. The sermons are thoroughly grounded in Scripture, each quoting the Bible frequently. Although his sermons dealt with substantive matters of Christian doctrine and experience, Wesley stated that he was not interested in setting forth in them philosophical speculation and complicated reasoning. The sermons were meant to help ordinary people deal with their commitment to Christ and its implications for their daily living. They remain worth our reading and study.

The *Explanatory Notes Upon the New Testament*, first published in 1755, contained Wesley's own translation of the New Testament and comments on the text drawn from both his own interpretation and the work of other scholars. Wesley claimed that his *Notes* were not intended to be an academic commentary but rather a study aid for "plain" people who "love the Word of God." We hasten to add, however, that Wesley was a biblical scholar who worked easily with the original language of the New Testament writers. The *Notes* and sermons are still recognized as doctrinal standards* in The United Methodist Church.

Wesley was also convinced that hymns were effective for Christian instruction. He had great respect for the hymns of the church and a special regard for those written by his brother Charles, which were permeated with scriptural teaching, stirred people's faith, and knit the Methodists together in a worshiping and ministering community. He referred to the first major Methodist hymnbook, *A Collection of Hymns for the Use of the People Called Methodists* (1780), as "a little body of experimental and practical divinity." From the earliest days of the movement to the present, Methodism has been known for its music and singing.

Published sermons, a commentary on the New Testament, and hymns were viewed by Wesley as means to convey the message of the gospel, to provide spiritual nourishment, and to empower people to live holy lives. They contain the marrow of Wesley's theology. Before we examine the main themes of his theology, we need to say something about the sources on which it was based.

The Sources of Wesley's Theology

Wesley did not think that he was introducing anything new or innovative in his interpretation of the Christian faith. He accepted and used theological approaches and methods that already existed in the Church of England in the eighteenth century. Among these were reliance on Scripture, tradition, reason, and experience as the main sources for understanding what a Christian and the Christian community should be and do. We must say something about each of these sources.

1. **Scripture.** Wesley considered the Bible to be the primary source for Christian belief and life. He wrote, "I will not, I dare not vary from this book, either in great things or small. I have no power to dispense with one jot or tittle of what is contained therein. I am determined to be a Bible Christian, not almost but altogether" (Sermon, "Causes of the Inefficacy of Christianity," 1787). Of course, Wesley did not mean that there were no other books worthy of the Christian's reading and study. He was an avid reader of a wide variety of literature, which he devoured on every possible occasion.

Wesley was persuaded, however, that the Bible was the book of utmost importance for him and for every Christian who took the faith seriously. Therefore he immersed himself in its language, stories, images, and themes, making it central to his daily study and medita-

25

tion. All his basic theological convictions were rooted in the Scriptures; and he constantly appealed to them in his preaching, teaching, and disputing about religious matters. The other three sources, that is, tradition, reason, and experience, were necessary to interpret the Bible, to assist Christians to understand it, and to put its message into practice.

Wesley was satisfied that the Bible was authoritative. It was inspired by God and should be read prayerfully with the assistance of the Holy Spirit. Ordinarily, each biblical text should be taken in its plain sense unless it would be absurd to do so. Texts should only be read and interpreted in the context in which they appear. It is easy, Wesley held, to pervert the meaning of a text by not paying attention to the verses that precede and follow it and by ignoring the place of any particular text within the whole message of the Bible.

2. **Tradition.** Wesley had both admiration and love for the history of the church. The Epworth rectory, his schooling at Oxford, and his study of the great women and men of church history made an important impression on his own thinking about Christianity. He was especially devoted to what he called "Christian antiquity," the religion of "the primitive church," the church of the earliest centuries. He consulted many early Christian writers because he found them faithful interpreters of the Scriptures. He thought their views worthy of consideration by Christians of every age.

One of the best illustrations of Wesley's commitment to tradition was his editing and publishing a fifty-volume work titled *A Christian Library,* a selection of readings from Christian authors from the second century to his own day. He encouraged his followers to learn from these earlier faithful efforts and wisdom. He was also devoted to *The Book of Common Prayer,* * which originated in the sixteenth century and contained the prayers and liturgies of the Church of England, including a cycle of daily Morning and Evening Prayer with psalms and other Scripture passages.

3. **Reason.** The eighteenth century is known as the Age of Reason, a time when it was believed that truth could only be known through reason, observation, and scientific experiment. It was the period of Deism,* a movement popular in England that attempted to construct

a religion based on reason and natural law. The Deists rejected revelation and were skeptical about the authority of Scripture and the traditional theology of the church. While acknowledging the existence of a Supreme Being, they doubted the possibility of miracles, the deity of Christ, and Jesus' death as a remedy for sin. Wesley opposed Deism because he believed it tampered with the central truths of Christianity.

John Wesley found himself caught between two opinions in the matter of reason and religion. On the one hand were those who did not sufficiently appreciate reason as one of God's good gifts. They valued emotional intensity and undervalued reason, considering it the enemy of religion. Not so, Wesley argued. A maturing faith always seeks to be grounded in sound reason and understanding. Faith and reason are not adversaries. On the other hand were thinkers like the Deists, who overvalued reason and denied revelation as a source of truth. Wesley argued that even though reason is a divine gift and indispensable for studying Scripture and analyzing Christian tradition, it has its limits in explaining the mysteries of God's being and acts. By itself, reason cannot produce faith, hope, or love and, therefore, it cannot give happiness.

Wesley tried to walk a fine line between these two extremes. Reason must not be either undervalued or overvalued. Reason and religion are compatible, and Wesley tried to convince Methodists and their critics that faith and thought were legitimate partners. He wrote, "It is a fundamental principle with us [Methodists] that to renounce reason is to renounce religion, that religion and reason go hand in hand, and that all irrational religion is false religion" (A Letter to the Rev. Dr. Rutherforth, 1768).

4. **Experience.** Wesley was constantly concerned about the role of experience in Christian theology. He was afraid that his followers would become satisfied with a spiritually stagnant orthodoxy that had none of the vitality and power of a personal relationship with God. In one of his most quoted comments he observed:

> I am not afraid that the people called Methodists should ever cease to exist, either in Europe or America. But I am afraid, lest they should only exist as a dead sect, having the form of religion without the power.
> *(Thoughts Upon Methodism, 1786)*

27

Throughout his ministry Wesley was critical of anyone whose religion consisted only of external forms or who mistakenly believed that he or she could earn God's favor by simply having the right theology, attending worship, receiving the sacraments, or occasionally giving something to the poor. He tried to convince them that true religion depends on God's grace and is blessed by a vital sense of God's presence.

The presence of God, Wesley maintained, is experienced by the believer in two ways. We have an outward experience of God as we observe God at work in nature and in the lives of other people. We also have an inward experience of God, by which we sense the divine presence working in our lives, assuring us that we are God's children and leading us to be more conformed to the image of Christ by walking in his justice, mercy, and truth. God's presence brings an inner consciousness of love, joy, and peace. If it is authentic, it is also attended by a change in the believer's behavior and actions.

For his emphasis on religious experience Wesley was branded an "enthusiast"* by some of his critics. They accused him of promoting dangerously unregulated and misdirected religious emotion. Wesley denied that he promoted disordered and misleading religious emotionalism. He recognized that genuine religious experience was disciplined by Scripture, tradition, and reason. Wesley was usually wary of emotional excesses and counseled his people to be cautious of unscriptural and irrational fanaticism. Yet he knew the importance of religious experience. He knew that people yearn to know God's presence at the deepest levels of their lives and that God seeks to come to them in a personal relationship.

We will come back to these four sources—Scripture, tradition, reason, and experience—which some call "the Wesleyan quadrilateral,"* in the last chapter when we speak about United Methodism's contemporary theological task.

The Main Themes of Wesley's Theology

Six main themes are central to Wesley's preaching and writing. They also appear prominently in the hymns of Charles Wesley. They are the problem of sin, prevenient grace, justification by faith, new birth, assurance, and holiness of heart and life. What did Wesley mean by each of these?

1. **The problem of sin.*** According to Wesley, human beings are created in the image of God *(Genesis 1:27)* and are intended to live in harmony with God and one another. Originally, they were given an ability to judge right from wrong. Their life was organized around love. They were free to make choices regarding their destiny. They were "at full liberty" to enjoy God and the rest of creation. As a result, they were happy.

Something went horribly wrong with the human situation, however. As Wesley studied the Bible, investigated history, observed what was happening around him, and looked deeply within himself, he recognized that there was a serious discrepancy between what God intended human beings to be and what they really are. He referred to this problem as "the loathsome leprosy of sin" *(Genesis 6:5; Romans 3:23).*

Sin, the awful state in which men, women, young people, and children live, is manifest in at least two ways. First, we are guilty of offenses against God. Some are outright atheists or hold God in contempt. Others forget God by ignoring worship, prayer, the sacraments, and the Bible. Others yield to idolatry, loving things more than their Creator and elevating their own desires above any intention to do God's will. They substitute the love of money, power, ease, and pleasure for the love of God. They are "unhinged" from God. Sin turns them away from God and turns them in on themselves *(Isaiah 31:8-14).*

Second, and inseparable from their offenses against God, they offend their neighbors, the neighbor being any and every other human being. They exercise anger, "ingratitude, revenge, hatred, envy, malice, uncharitableness," indifference and neglect. Not only are they chargeable with personal sins, but they are also participants in large-scale systems of wickedness that oppose God's will, such as making war and oppressing the poor *(1 John 3:15-17).*

Sin is a universal disease that saps human life. Wesley observed,

> Our body, soul, and spirit, are infected, overspread, consumed, with [this] most fatal leprosy. We are all over, within and without, in the eyes of God, full of diseases, and wounds, and putrifying sores.
>
> (Sermon, "The One Thing Needful," 1734)

The great need of all of us is the Divine Physician, who can restore our souls to health and renew God's image in us (Sermons, "Original Sin," 1759; "On the Fall of Man," 1782; "The Deceitfulness of the Human Heart," 1790).

2. **Prevenient grace.*** The answer to the desperate condition of sinners is divine grace, God's unmerited, unearned, undeserved love at work in the world. Wesley referred to one aspect of this love as "prevenient grace." The term literally means "the grace that comes before." It might be more helpful to think of it as "preparing grace," the grace that prepares us for God's forgiveness and a holy life. Wesley believed that prevenient grace through the work of the Holy Spirit is present in all people. He spoke of it as "free in all, and free for all" (Sermon, "Free Grace," 1739).

God's prevenient, preparing grace awakens us to the seriousness of our sinful condition, shows us the way to new life, frees us to accept God's offer of pardon and reconciliation, and moves us to repentance and change. Without prevenient grace we are not liberated from the influence of sin to respond to God's offer of forgiveness and new life *(1 John 4:19).*

We need to say something here about the notion of predestination,* an issue that was controversial in Wesley's time. In his day, predestination meant that sin had completely destroyed the freedom of the human will. Since human beings were totally unable to respond to any offer of divine pardon, God determined before their birth those who were to be forgiven by grace and granted new life and those who were not.

Wesley found this type of predestinarian theology unacceptable, first of all because it was not scriptural. He also listed several other objections. For example, predestination made preaching the gospel unnecessary. Why proclaim the good news if God has already chosen before their birth those who are to be pardoned? Furthermore, predestination discourages living the holy life. If people believe they are predestined, they are likely to feel no need to become more mature in their faith; and their zeal to do good works will be subdued. Finally, predestination is a blasphemous idea because it misrepresents God. Instead of the compassionate, merciful, loving, and just God of Scripture, it suggests a tyrant who cruelly forecloses any response to saving grace by predetermining who is forgiven and who is irretrievably lost (Sermon, "Free Grace," 1739).

God's prevenient grace restores to everyone the freedom to respond to God *(John 3:16)*. One of Charles Wesley's hymns speaks of the Wesleyan notion of prevenient grace:

> Come, sinners, to the gospel feast;
> let every soul be Jesus' guest.
> Ye need not one be left behind,
> for God hath bid all humankind.
>
> Sent by my Lord, on you I call;
> the invitation is to all.
> Come, all the world! Come, sinner thou!
> All things in Christ are ready now.
>
> Come, all ye souls by sin oppressed,
> ye restless wanderers after rest;
> ye poor, and maimed, and halt, and blind,
> in Christ a hearty welcome find.
>
> My message as from God receive;
> ye all may come to Christ and live.
> O let his love your hearts constrain,
> nor suffer him to die in vain.
>
> This is the time, no more delay!
> This is the Lord's accepted day.
> Come thou, this moment, at his call,
> and live for him who died for all.
> ("Come, Sinners, to the Gospel Feast,"
> *The United Methodist Hymnal*, 339)

3. **Justification by faith.*** God's prevenient grace prepares us for new life. God's grace also accepts us and provides the healing we need. It breaks the hold that sin has on us and "sets [sin's] prisoner free."

John Wesley was heir to one of the principal ideas of the Protestant Reformation, justification by faith, an idea that is prominent in Scripture. Justification considers how unrighteous people stand before the righteous God. By their offenses against God and their neighbors, the unrighteous deserve God's judgment and wrath. They are unable to justify themselves because on their own they cannot live a holy life. Therefore they are constantly dependent on God's accepting and pardoning love *(Romans 5:1-5)*.

Justification is vitally linked with Jesus Christ in whom God is at work for our salvation. Jesus is the "God-man," truly God and truly human, whose main work is to reconcile us to God. A nativity hymn of Charles Wesley testifies to the event of God's coming among us in Christ and to the salvation he brings:

> Christ, by highest heaven adored;
>   Christ, the everlasting Lord;
> late in time behold him come,
>   off-spring of a virgin's womb.
> Veiled in flesh the God-head see;
>   hail th'incarnate Deity,
> pleased with us in flesh to dwell,
>   Jesus, our Emmanuel.
> Hark! the herald angels sing,
>   "Glory to the new-born King!"
>
> Hail the heaven-born Prince of Peace!
>   Hail the Sun of Righteousness!
> Light and life to all he brings,
>   risen with healing in his wings.
> Mild he lays his glory by,
>   born that we no more may die,
> born to raise us from the earth,
>   born to give us second birth.
> Hark! the herald angels sing,
>   "Glory to the new-born King!"
> ("Hark! the Herald Angels Sing,"
>   *The United Methodist Hymnal*, 240)

The life, death, and resurrection of Jesus are intimately related to our justification. Wesley regarded Jesus as our Prophet, Priest, and King. By his life and teaching, Jesus the Prophet *(Luke 7:26)* disclosed to all the whole will of God. By his death, Jesus the Priest *(Hebrews 7:15-17)* offered himself as a sacrifice for sin and acts as our Mediator, the Righteous One acting on behalf of the unrighteous. By his resurrection and continuing presence among us, Jesus is the King who reigns until he has brought all things under his dominion *(Philippians 2:9-11; Revelation 17:14)*. God in Christ does something for us that we cannot do for ourselves (A Letter to a Roman Catholic, 1749).

We are justified, pardoned, and reconciled to God on the basis of our faith. What is the nature of this faith? Wesley was adamant in stating that it is more than embracing certain facts. It is not simply believing in the existence of God or believing that Jesus is the Savior of the human race. Genuine faith is total trust, reliance, and confidence in the grace of God evident in the person and work of Christ as Prophet, Priest, and King (Sermons, "The Scripture Way of Salvation," 1765; "On Faith, Hebrews 11:6," 1788; "The Lord Our Righteousness," 1765).

4. **New Birth.*** Wesley emphasized the importance of experiencing God's accepting, justifying grace by faith. Justification by faith and new birth are inseparable. For purposes of analysis and discussion, however, Wesley thought the two could be distinguished. Justification, he held, is the work God does for us. The new birth *(John 3:1-10; 2 Corinthians 5:17)* is the work God does *in us*. In his words,

> I believe [the new birth] to be an inward thing; a change from inward wickedness to inward goodness; an entire change of our inmost nature from the image of the devil . . . to the image of God; a change from the love of the creature to the love of the Creator; from earthly and sensual to heavenly and holy affections,—in a word, a change from the tempers of the spirits of darkness to those of the angels of God in heaven.
>
> *(Journal, September 13, 1739)*

To help people understand the nature of the new birth, Wesley compared it to natural human birth. The unborn has eyes but cannot see, ears but cannot hear, and has other undeveloped senses. The unborn has no knowledge or understanding of things beyond the womb. As soon as the child is born, however, light, sound, and sensory experiences are newly perceived. Life becomes entirely different. So it is with newborn Christians. They are awakened to new life. Their spiritual eyes are opened to recognize God's presence and love. They hear God speaking words of comfort and challenge. All their spiritual senses are enlivened, and they are prepared for living in fellowship with God and growing into the image of Christ. New birth is the result of the Holy Spirit's work. Wesley was sure of that. However, he was equally convinced that no one knows precisely the manner in which the Spirit brings it into being (Sermon, "The New Birth," 1760).

Wesley was persuaded that the purpose of new birth is not merely to give people an extraordinary experience of God and to fill them with good feelings. Furthermore, it is not an end in itself. Rather, the new birth is the beginning of a new life of holiness in which people are more sensitive to the presence of God, the circumstances of their neighbors, and the need to live the holy life.

According to Wesley, there are three marks of the new birth: faith, hope, and love. The *faith* of people born of God is "a sure trust and confidence in God that through the merits of Christ" their sins are forgiven and they are reconciled to God's favor. Their *hope* is the testimony of the Holy Spirit that they are truly God's children. Sin no longer holds power over them. The third mark is *love*, a genuine, deep, and growing love for God. Wesley added:

> The necessary fruit of this love of God is love of our neighbor, of every soul which God hath made; not excepting our enemies, not excepting those who are now "despitefully using and persecuting us"; a love whereby we love every[one] as ourselves—as we love our own souls.
> (Sermon, "The Marks of the New Birth," 1748)

Wesley's views on the relationship between the new birth and baptism are important and instructive. In two places he dealt extensively with this issue, a tract titled, "A Treatise on Baptism" (1758), and a sermon, "The New Birth" (1760). The baptism of infants and adults was significant for Wesley. Baptism was well established in the Bible and in the general practice of the church since its beginning. He had no reservations about infant baptism. Wesley was convinced that God's saving grace was conveyed to infants in baptism. It was the beginning of the Christian life. However, he was persuaded that many, if not most, people turned away from God in the years following their baptism as infants and needed the inward change that God works through the atonement of Christ and the empowerment of the

Holy Spirit. They needed new birth. United Methodism approved an official statement on baptism titled, "By Water and the Spirit," at its 1996 General Conference that incorporates Wesley's views and places them in the wider context of contemporary discipleship.

5. **Assurance.*** Those who, by faith, receive the accepting grace of God and are given new life become God's children. They do not have to wonder about their status. The Scriptures teach (especially *Romans 8:16*) and the experience of Christian people confirms, Wesley said, that the Spirit of God bears constant witness in believers that they enjoy a new standing with God. This is called the "witness" or "testimony of the Holy Spirit." Wesley wrote:

> The testimony of the [Holy] Spirit is an inward impression on the soul, whereby the Spirit of God directly "witnesses to my spirit that I am a child of God; that Jesus Christ hath loved me, and given Himself for me; that all my sins are blotted out, and I, even I, am reconciled to God."
> (Sermon, "The Witness of the Spirit, I," 1746)

As elsewhere, Wesley confessed his inability to explain the manner in which the Spirit worked this witness. It was another mystery. He said:

> I do not mean . . . that the Spirit of God testifies this by an outward voice; no, nor always by an inward voice, although he may do this sometimes. Nor do I suppose that he always applies to the heart (though he often may) one or more texts of scripture. But he so works upon the soul by his immediate influence, and by a strong though inexplicable operation, that the stormy wind and troubled waves subside, and there is a sweet calm; the heart resting as in the arms of Jesus, and the sinner being clearly satisfied that God is reconciled, that all his "iniquities are forgiven, and his sins covered."
> (Sermon, "The Witness of the Spirit, II," 1767)

Charles Wesley expressed this view of assurance in one of his hymns:

> No condemnation now I dread;
> Jesus, and all in him, is mine;

Alive in him, my living Head,
  and clothed in righteousness divine,
bold I approach th'eternal throne,
  and claim the crown,
through Christ my own.
("And Can It Be That I Should Gain,"
  The United Methodist Hymnal, 363)

The witness or testimony of the Holy Spirit on which the concept of Christian assurance was based should never be a matter of inappropriate pride. It is never something to flaunt. It is simply another gift of grace that provides the base on which further growth in holiness and ministry takes place. Its immediate consequences are the fruits of the Spirit: love, joy, peace, patience, gentleness, kindness, faithfulness, generosity, and self-control *(Galatians 5:22-23)*.

6. **Holiness of heart and life.*** The final and culminating theme of Wesley's theology is holiness of heart and life, what the biblical writers and other Christian thinkers have sometimes called sanctification. Throughout his life, Wesley was devoted to holy living. He had learned its importance as a child in the Epworth rectory. His reading and study of the Scriptures and the great devotional writers of the church had confirmed the notion that it is essential to the authentic Christian life. His sermons and other writings are saturated with explaining the nature of holiness and exhorting people by the grace of God to seek it and practice it. He underscored its significance in his comparison of the structure of the Christian faith to a house. Imagine, he said, that the porch of the house is repentance. You cannot get into the house without going onto the porch. The door of the house is justification by faith (pardon, forgiveness, reconciliation with God). You cannot get into the house without going through the door. But the house itself, for which the porch and door are means of access, is holiness of heart and life *(The Principles of Methodism Farther Explained*, 1746). Christianity is primarily about the holy life. What then is the essence of this holiness?

Holiness has two main aspects: inward and outward, or in other words, personal and social holiness. Although these two are inseparable from each other, for purposes of describing them we need to examine each one individually.

Inward holiness involves total commitment to God, singleness of intention, centering one's life completely on God. It includes believing in, trusting, loving, worshiping, imitating, and obeying God. It consists of constant reliance on God's grace and using the gifts God gives to become what God intends us to be. We describe some of these gifts in the next chapter. Inward holiness is impossible without God's sustaining grace made available in these gifts. Inward holiness has to do with examining our lives, repenting of our sins, and cultivating the gifts of the Spirit in us. It is about seeking God's presence to deepen our faith, hope, and love. Genuine, lasting peace and joy are the results of the holy life.

Outward holiness entails the manner in which we show our love for God in our love for our neighbors, remembering that the neighbor is **anyone** and **everyone** else. Following Scripture, Wesley held that Christianity is essentially a social religion. To make it a solitary religion is to destroy it. It cannot exist without living and conversing with other people. To hide it is impossible. "Sure it is," he wrote, "that a secret, unobserved religion cannot be the religion of Jesus Christ. Whatever religion can be concealed is not Christianity" (Sermon, "Upon Our Lord's Sermon on the Mount, IV," 1748).

In many places in his writings Wesley specified the ways in which outward holiness should be evident in response to our neighbors. There were unholy thoughts and acts to avoid, such as envy, hasty judgment, pride, anger, injustice, greed, quarreling, intemperance, and neglecting others' needs. There were likewise holy habits to be exercised in our relationships with others, such as patience, kindness, generosity, forgiveness, justice, self-denial, sacrifice, and desiring the best for our neighbors. We should love not only God but also use all the means God provides to love others as well *(Luke 10:27)*. In a later chapter we will be discussing "works of mercy," Wesley's phrase for mission and ministry to others.

A distinguishing feature of Wesley's views on holiness was his advocacy of Christian perfection as the goal of the holy life *(Matthew 5:48; 1 John 4:18)*. There was considerable misunderstanding and controversy about this idea in Wesley's day and later. It is generally neglected in many of the "Wesleyan" churches today. One of the places it surfaces is at United Methodist annual conferences, when clergy candidates are publicly asked the traditional questions, "Are you going on to perfection? Do you expect to be made perfect in love in this life? Are you earnestly striving after it?"

The perfection Wesley envisioned is not freedom from ignorance, error, and temptation. These are unavoidable by the most devoted Christian. He meant that with God's help the Christian could possess purity of heart, the Spirit's greatest gift, by which love becomes the controlling affection of our life, we have the mind of Christ, and we walk as he walked (Sermons, "On Love," 1737; "Christian Perfection," 1741; "On Perfection," 1784). In a familiar hymn of Charles Wesley we pray for the perfection of holy love in us:

> Finish, then, thy new creation;
>   pure and spotless let us be.
> Let us see thy great salvation
>   perfectly restored in thee;
> changed from glory into glory,
>   till in heaven we take our place,
> till we cast our crowns before thee,
>   lost in wonder, love, and praise.
> ("Love Divine, All Loves Excelling,"
> *The United Methodist Hymnal,* 384)

Holiness of heart and life, with its goal of perfect love, is nurtured by "works of piety" and "works of mercy." We turn to these topics in the next two chapters.

Some Questions for Reflection and Discussion

1. Although we are reluctant to think of ourselves as "theologians," each of us thinks about our Christian faith; and we try to act on the basis of what we think is appropriate Christian action. So, by our thoughts, words, and acts we embody a theology. How do you use the "Wesleyan quadrilateral" (Scripture, tradition, reason, and experience) in the formulation of your theology and decision-making?

2. *The United Methodist Hymnal* has sections of hymns and prayers on "Prevenient Grace" (337–360), "Justifying Grace" (361–381), and "Sanctifying and Perfecting Grace" (382–536). How do these hymns help you to understand these three major emphases of Wesleyan theology?

3. We have noted that one of the serious theological debates of Wesley's day concerned predestination. What were Wesley's arguments against predestination mentioned earlier in this chapter? How is predestination understood today?

4. How can Wesley's idea of "holiness of heart and life," especially his notion of Christian perfection, become a reality in your life?

3

CHAPTER

"WORKS OF PIETY"

Spiritual Formation in the Wesleyan Tradition

We rarely stand still when it comes to our faith and relationship to God. Faith by its very nature seeks greater depth and understanding. It either receives the nourishment and cultivation it needs to grow, or it begins to wither in the face of the changes and challenges of daily living.

One of the most impressive things about John Wesley was his struggle to become the person he thought God wanted him to be, someone who was holy in heart and life. He was not a Christian theologian and church leader who lived above the world's conflicts and turmoil. He was realistic about the obstacles, doubts, failures, and crises with which faithful people must cope. He constantly wrestled with them himself. At times he possessed the trusting, confident faith that ought to characterize the Christian life. At other times he felt spiritually destitute and claimed he was not a Christian at all. Wesley was well enough acquainted with a wide variety of Christians to know that they too were subject to moments of elation and times of despair. He was aware that the Christian life has its peaks and valleys.

Wesley was specific about the threats to holiness of heart and life. He realized, for example, that all Christians have to contend with temptations of various kinds, some of them compelling. They have to deal with diversions that "uncenter the soul from God." Words and deeds that unjustly injure our neighbors and neglect of the neighbors' needs are also a serious menace to walking with Christ. Christians must be vigilant so that they do not backslide from their commitment to grow into the image of Jesus.

Since they are never exempt from sin in their lives, Christians understand the importance of repentance and the continuing need of God's forgiveness. If they are going on to higher holiness and maturity, they realize their need of God's sustaining grace. God's preparing (prevenient) grace makes them ready for new life in Christ. God's accepting (justifying) grace initiates them into it. Then, God's sustaining (sanctifying) and perfecting grace supports, encourages, and empowers them.

The Means of Grace

Wesley discovered several ways in which God provides sustaining grace. The influence of parents, the study of Scripture, reading Christian thinkers from the early church to his day, and his own practice of a disciplined Christian life mapped out for him the main routes by which God works to nurture holiness. Wesley called them "means of grace" and exhorted his people to make full use of them for spiritual growth and ministry. We offer the following description of some of the principal means of grace enumerated by Wesley. The list is not exhaustive but constitutes the core of his thought.

1. **Searching the Scriptures.** We noted in the last chapter the importance of the Bible for Wesley as a source of his theology. It is the Christian's privilege and duty, he thought, to "search the scriptures." The Bible contains the basic message of God's grace and is the primary guide for holy living *(2 Timothy 3:16-17)*.

Wesley read the Bible daily, ordinarily early in the day or late in the evening when he was free to devote concentrated attention to its message. He read it systematically, usually following the readings prescribed in the Church of England's *Book of Common Prayer.* He preferred this to a more haphazard approach, though he confessed that on rare occasions when he was spiritually "distressed," he randomly opened the Bible looking for divine comfort and direction.

It was Wesley's custom to offer practical advice to his people on a variety of topics. It is not surprising to discover, therefore, that he made precise suggestions for reading the Scriptures. There were six. (1) If possible, set apart a little time in the morning and evening every day for Bible reading. (2) It is advisable to read a chapter from both the Old Testament and the New Testament. (3) Read with a single purpose—to know the will of God. (4) Look for the connections between the passage of Scripture being read and the fundamental ideas of Christian faith. (5) Prayerfully seek the guidance and instruction of the Holy Spirit as you read. (6) Resolve to put into practice what God teaches you in your reading and study *(Explanatory Notes Upon the Old Testament,* 1765).

While personal Bible study is important, Wesley also expected people to benefit from the scriptural message as it was read at family worship, preached and taught in parish churches, and studied and interpreted in society and class meetings. Among the rules for Methodists was the admonition that they attend the "ministry of the Word, either read or expounded." The church is not the church without the faithful reading and proclamation of the Bible. He was well aware, however, that in many parish churches the biblical message was not proclaimed with the insight and power it deserved. Nor was it heard in many communities by those who needed most to know its words of judgment and healing. That is why he felt driven to preach the gospel outside the parish church building and to organize people to hear the Bible preached and sung in biblically based hymns in Methodist meetings.

The Wesleyan respect for Scripture and its power as the Word of God when read faithfully is set forth in one of Charles Wesley's hymns:

> Whether the Word be preached or read,
>   no saving benefit I gain
> from empty sounds or letters dead;
>   unprofitable all and vain,
> unless by faith thy word I hear
>   and see its heavenly character.
>
> If God enlighten through his Word,
>   I shall my kind Enlightener bless;
> but void and naked of my Lord,
>   what are all verbal promises?
> Nothing to me, till faith divine
>   inspire, inspeak, and make them mine.
>
> Jesus, the appropriating grace
>   'tis thine on sinners to bestow,
> Open mine eyes to see thy face,

open my heart thyself to know.
And then I through thy Word obtain
sure present, and eternal gain.
("Whether the Word Be Preached or Read,"
The United Methodist Hymnal, 595)

The United Methodist Church follows Wesley's devotion to the Bible. It clearly announces in *The Book of Discipline* (pages 75–76):

The biblical authors, illumined by the Holy Spirit, bear witness that in Christ the world is reconciled to God. The Bible bears authentic testimony to God's self-disclosure in the life, death, and resurrection of Jesus Christ as well as in God's work of creation, in the pilgrimage of Israel, and in the Holy Spirit's ongoing activity in human history.

As we open our minds and hearts to the Word of God through the words of human beings inspired by the Holy Spirit, faith is born and nourished, our understanding is deepened, and the possibilities for transforming the world become apparent to us. . . .

We properly read Scripture within the believing community, informed by the tradition of that community. We interpret individual texts in light of their place in the Bible as a whole. . . .

While we acknowledge the primacy of Scripture in theological reflection, our attempts to grasp its meaning always involve tradition, experience, and reason. Like Scripture, these may become creative vehicles of the Holy Spirit as they function within the Church. They quicken our faith, open our eyes to the wonder of God's love, and clarify our understanding.

The intention here is consistent with Wesley's teaching. Our situation today, however, is quite different from Wesley's. Our study and interpretation of the Bible have been enhanced by resources that Wesley never anticipated. Archaeology, discoveries of older biblical manuscripts, research on the biblical languages, new translations, and other developments have created a vast amount of information about the Bible and its message. Wesley's resources were less complex, and we can only guess what he would have made of biblical scholarship today. While we can imagine that he would remind us that these new tools have not changed the basic message of the Bible, he would probably be appalled by the biblical illiteracy that is so widespread in the modern church. "How do you expect faith and holiness to grow unless you search the Scriptures?" he might ask.

2. **Prayer.** Since the Christian life is lived in relationship with God through Jesus Christ, Wesley believed that prayer is essential. It is one of God's most important gifts to keep us connected to the One who steadfastly loves us and whose grace is necessary to sustain us *(Psalm 40:1-3)*. It is "the grand means of drawing near to God." The Christian exercises love for God by praying "without ceasing" *(1 Thessalonians 5:17)*. On the other hand, the absence of prayer, he believed, is the single most serious cause of spiritual drought in the life of a Christian. Therefore, Wesley advised his people to pray continually. A stanza of one of Charles Wesley's hymns reinforces this necessity and reads in part:

> Still let me seek to thee for aid,
> To thee my weakness show;
> Hang on thy arm alone,
> With self-distrusting care,
> And deeply in the spirit groan
> The never-ceasing prayer.

Wesley never expected the Methodists to do what he did not do himself. His practice of prayer is illustrative. His private diaries show that he prayed daily. Early in the morning, late in the evening, and often at other times during the day, Wesley engaged in private prayer and found it a source of great strength (Journal, May 27, 1738). He also prayed with others at morning and evening worship at the parish church or cathedral and in Methodist society and class meetings. He discovered early in life that praying with others, in the family, in small groups, and in the larger fellowship of a congregation are important means to offer praise, to seek God's fortifying grace, and to ask God's blessing on others.

How should we pray? Wesley was convinced that prayer can be of our own making (he called it "extemporary") or we can profitably use the multitude of prayers in the church's prayer books and devotional literature. Wesley, of course, extensively used the prayers and liturgies in the Church of England's *Book of Common Prayer*, but he turned to the devotional readings and prayers of other Christians as well, such as Jeremy Taylor and William Law. While there were some in his day who thought that composing one's own prayers was "irregular" and foolish, the problem of our time seems just the opposite. Many people feel we are not really praying if we use the written prayers of the church or someone else, but this is not a Wesleyan attitude. Wesley felt that it is difficult to carry on a vital prayer life simply using the prayers we make up (Journal, January 2, 1737).

Perhaps it was for that reason that Wesley published collections of prayers. These included prayers for every day of the week, prayers for families, and prayers for children. Although he had no children of his own, he had great affection for them and used every opportunity to encourage them to become faithful followers of Jesus. In the preface to a prayerbook for children he wrote:

> A Lover of your soul has here drawn up a few Prayers, in order to assist you in that great duty. Be sure that you do not omit, at least morning and evening, to present yourself upon your knees before God.
> (*Prayers for Children*, 1772)

One of the prayers for children reads:

> Vouchsafe, O Lord, to bless my father and mother, and all my relations, with the fear of thy name. Bless them in their souls and bodies; perfect them in every good word and work, and be thou their guide unto death. Bless my friends, forgive my enemies; and grant to all . . . the knowledge and love of thee. Have mercy upon all who are afflicted in mind, body, or estate. Give them patience under their sufferings, and a happy issue out of all their afflictions; and receive them and me at last into thy blessed kingdom, for Jesus Christ's sake. Amen.
> (*Prayers for Children*, 1772)

Methodists have never simply **said** their prayers. They have also sung them. Our hymnals have been full of prayerful songs addressed to the triune God. Here is one of Charles Wesley's hymns:

Maker, in whom we live,
  in whom we are and move,
the glory, power, and praise receive
  for thy creating love.
Let all the angel throng
  give thanks to God on high,
while earth repeats the joyful song
  and echoes to the sky.

Incarnate Deity,
  let all the ransomed race
render in thanks their lives to thee
  for thy redeeming grace.
The grace to sinners showed
  ye heavenly choirs proclaim,
and cry, "Salvation to our God,
  salvation to the Lamb!"

Spirit of Holiness,
  let all thy saints adore
thy sacred energy, and bless
  thine heart-renewing power.
Not angel tongues can tell
  thy love's ecstatic height,
the glorious joy unspeakable,
  the beatific sight.

Eternal, Triune God,
  let all the hosts above,
let all on earth below record
  and dwell upon thy love.
When heaven and earth are fled
  before thy glorious face,
sing all the saints thy love hath made
  thine everlasting praise.
      ("Maker, in Whom We Live,"
      The United Methodist Hymnal, 88)

   3. **Fasting.** When most of us think about fasting, it is usually because it is time to lose some weight. When John Wesley thought

about it, he viewed it as a spiritual discipline whose purpose was not to reduce the intake of calories but to enhance the holy life.

Wesley was convinced that fasting, abstaining from food or drink, was a practice firmly grounded in the Bible. People in Old Testament times fasted (*Ezra 8:23*). So did Jesus and his followers (*Matthew 4:2; Acts 13:3*), and Wesley saw no reason why modern Christians should not follow the same pattern. His plan of fasting sometimes allowed for limited eating and drinking. He found that fasting advanced holiness. In his early ministry he fasted with others on Wednesdays and Fridays, though later he seems to have done so only on Fridays. He expected his followers to do the same. In a sermon published in 1789, "Causes of the Inefficacy of Christianity," he criticized his followers because too many were not keeping the regular Friday fast.

Why was fasting important to Wesley? He listed several reasons, some of which were (1) it is an expression of sorrow for sin; (2) it is a special sign of penitence for the sin of indulging in excessive eating and drinking; and (3) it is a help to prayer because it allows the person fasting to set apart a larger time for praying. He advised that fasting should be

> done unto the Lord, with our eye singly fixed on Him. Let our intention here-in be this, and this alone, to glorify our Father which is in heaven; to express our sorrow and shame for our manifold transgressions of his holy law; to wait for an increase of purifying grace, drawing our affections to things above; to add seriousness and earnestness to our prayers; to avert the wrath of God, and to obtain all the great and precious promises which he hath made to us in Jesus Christ.
> (Sermon, "Upon Our Lord's Sermon on the Mount, VII," 1748)

Caution must be exercised in the practice of fasting, Wesley stated. Extreme fasting was to be avoided, and for some in fragile health it might be dangerous. In the same sermon he cautioned:

> Yea, the body may sometimes be afflicted too much, so as to be unfit for the works of our calling. This also we are to diligently guard against; for we ought to preserve our health, as a good gift of God.
> (Sermon, "Upon Our Lord's Sermon on the Mount, VII," 1748)

He hastened to add that fasting would be enhanced by accompanying it with giving to the poor.

4. **The Lord's Supper.** United Methodists usually celebrate the Lord's Supper once a month or four times a year. John Wesley would have been mystified by this. After all, he communed an average every four to five days during his adult life. He claimed that the Lord's Supper is absolutely indispensable in the Christian life. He wrote:

> Let everyone . . . who has either any desire to please God, or any love of his own soul, obey God and consult the good of his own soul by [receiving Communion] every time he can; like the first Christians, [for] whom the [Lord's Supper] was a constant part of the Lord's day's service.
>
> (Sermon, "The Duty of Constant Communion," 1787)

What did this sacrament mean to Wesley? What happens when we come to the Lord's Table? He taught that the Lord's Supper is significant for three reasons.

First, it is a memorial or remembrance (*1 Corinthians 11:23-26*). It sets before us Christ's suffering and atoning death. With eyes of faith and by the power of the Holy Spirit, we transcend time and space and find ourselves at the foot of the cross. We remember that Christ died for us. Wesley confessed that this is a deep and holy mystery. Charles captured the substance of this idea in these words:

> Prince of Life, for Sinners slain,
>   Grant us Fellowship with Thee,
> Fain we would partake thy pain
>   Share thy mortal Agony,
> Give us now the dreadful Power,
>   Now bring back thy Dying Hour.
>
> Surely now the Prayer He hears:
>   Faith presents the Crucified!
> Lo! the wounded Lamb appears
>   Pierc'd his Feet, his Hands, his Side,
> Hangs our Hope on Yonder Tree,
>   Hangs, and bleeds to Death for me!

Second, the Lord's Supper is a way by which God conveys grace to the recipient (*John 6:27*). By the power of the Holy Spirit and through

48

our faith, Christ and the benefits of his death and resurrection are communicated to us. As we eat the bread and drink the cup, God "conveys into our souls all that spiritual grace, that righteousness, and peace, and joy in the Holy Ghost, which were purchased by the body of Christ once broken and the blood of Christ once shed for us" (Sermon, "The Means of Grace," 1746).

Again, the Wesleys were awed by how this takes place. Charles wrote:

> O the depth of love divine,
>   the unfathomable grace!
> Who shall say how bread and wine
>   God into us conveys!
> How the bread his flesh imparts,
>   how the wine transmits his blood,
> fills his faithful people's hearts
>   with all the life of God!
>   ("O the Depth of Love Divine,"
>   *The United Methodist Hymnal*, 627)

John Wesley believed that three types of grace can be conveyed in the Lord's Supper: prevenient grace (which he called "convincing grace"), justifying grace (which he called "converting grace"), and sustaining grace (which he termed "sanctifying grace").

Third, the Supper is also a pledge. It confirms and seals God's offer of salvation in Christ. When we come together to the Lord's Table, we are anticipating what is to take place in the future consummated kingdom of God, when we will all share in the complete fullness of God's life in joy and peace (*Matthew 26:26-29*).

Some may register excuses for staying away from the Lord's Supper. "I am unworthy," some may say. Wesley's reply was curt. We are all unworthy to receive any mercy from God, he said; "if we are not to receive the Lord's Supper till we are worthy of it, it is certain we ought never to receive it." Others may say, "I have no time to prepare for it." The only preparation necessary, he responded, is repentance, faith in Christ, and a sincere desire to amend your life. "Frequent communion lessens our reverence for the sacrament," some claim. On the contrary, he reasoned, regular communing confirms and increases our reverence for it. Yet another excuse is offered by some who say, "The sacrament has not benefited me as I thought it would." If you are properly prepared for it by trusting Christ, and receive it often, God has promised to bless you (Sermon, "The Duty of Constant Communion," 1787).

We can appreciate why Wesley urged people to receive the sacrament as often as possible. Not only is it the command of Christ, but it is a principal way God nourishes us for the journey of life.

5. **Christian Conference.** * One of the important means of grace is the gift of "Christian conference," opportunities of joining with others for worship, fellowship, and ministry (*Acts 2:44-47*). Spiritual growth is personal, but it is not private. Holiness of heart and life cannot be developed in isolation. We cannot be Christians in solitude. For that reason Wesley knew it was necessary to organize his people in a manner that encouraged their nurture and their ministry to others. Although he called this means of grace "Christian conference," it is clearer for our purposes to refer to it as Christian fellowship and conversation (*Minutes of Several Conversations Between The Rev. Mr. Wesley and Others*, 1791).

We have already noted that early in the Methodist movement Wesley formed societies, classes, and bands for the people who had been changed by God through his preaching. The societies were composed of men and women who came together weekly to pray, to sing, to hear scriptural preaching, and "to watch over one another in love" (*1 John 4:7*). Since Wesley considered Methodism a movement within the Church of England, the Methodist societies met on weekday mornings or evenings when, as we observed earlier, they did not compete with the regularly scheduled worship in the parish churches. Society meetings were usually led by the Wesleys or one of the lay preachers.

Wesley developed "General Rules" to discipline the life of the societies. These rules specified that anyone was eligible to join a society so long as the person had a desire "to flee from the wrath to come," wished to be forgiven of sin, and gave continuing evidence of serious commitment to the Christian faith and life by keeping them. The General Rules are still printed in *The Book of Discipline of The United Methodist Church*.

Classes were smaller groups within a society. Each class had about twelve members, met weekly, and was directed by a class leader who was a committed laywoman or layman. The responsibilities of the leader were

1. To see each person in [the] class once a week at the least; in order to receive what they are willing to give toward the relief of the poor;
   To inquire how their souls prosper;
   To advise, reprove, comfort, or exhort, as occasion may require.

2. To inform the Minister of any that are sick, or of any that walk disorderly and will not be reproved.
   (*The Nature, Design, and General Rules of the United Societies*, 1743)

The classes provided an intimate fellowship in which the members talked about their progress in holiness, including their concerns, temptations, and failings. In the classes they developed mutual love for one another and resolved to reach out to others in need in their communities. Class meetings still exist in some congregations of United Methodism, and it has been suggested that the church would be stronger and more effective if we once again incorporated the class model into our regular life.

Wesley's bands were groups of Christians who were deemed to be more spiritually mature. They usually had fewer members than the classes. Wesley's rules for the bands were rigorous, requiring, among other things:

1. To be at church, and at the Lord's table, every week, and at every public meeting of the bands.
2. To attend the ministry of the Word every morning, unless distance, business, or sickness prevent.
3. To use private prayer every day, and family prayer if you are the head of a family.
4. To read the Scriptures, and meditate thereon, at every vacant hour.
   And,
5. To observe as days of fasting or abstinence all Fridays in the year.
   (*Rules of the Band Societies*, 1738)

To be a Methodist, it was essential to be united with other Christians, worship and pray with them, care for them, and join with them in ministry to the world. In Charles Wesley's words, their prayer should be

Help us to help each other, Lord,
    each other's cross to bear;
let all their friendly aid afford,
    and feel each other's care.
("Jesus, United by Thy Grace,"
The United Methodist Hymnal, 561)

The Methodist societies, classes, and bands, though scattered throughout the land, were the major components in a connection* devised by Wesley. Another critical element was his formation of an annual conference of preachers, mostly lay men and women, who were the backbone of the Methodist leadership. They were Wesley's "assistants and helpers." As mentioned, beginning in 1744, Wesley met with these leaders to discuss theological issues, to plan mission strategy, and to appoint them to their preaching places for the ensuing year. This connectional structure has always been important. *The Book of Discipline* includes a section that describes "the connectional principle."

6. **Public worship.** Wesley assumed that every Christian recognized the importance of worship. People who were truly touched by God must use every occasion to offer their praise and open themselves to God's sustaining grace in family prayers, parish services, and Methodist meetings. In addition to these, Wesley designed two distinctive worship occasions in which people would experience special blessing: the Love Feast and the Covenant Service.

The Love Feast* was based on the practice of the early Christian community's eating together, as described in Acts 2:46: "with glad and generous hearts." Wesley drew on his experience with the Moravians, who used the Love Feast as a way of creating deeper Christian fellowship. These celebrations of Christian companionship were not a substitute for the Lord's Supper. They were times for Christians to testify about God's working in their lives, to praise God in singing, to pray for each other and the world, and to eat and drink together. In Wesley's day the food was simply "a little plain cake and water." He said that people rarely participated in them without being fed both the food "which perisheth" and the spiritual food "which endureth to everlasting life" (*A Plain Account of the People Called Methodists*, 1749).

There is a contemporary liturgy for the Love Feast in *The United Methodist Book of Worship* (page 581), and hymns for a Love Feast are suggested in *The United Methodist Hymnal* (see Index of Topics and Categories, page 947).

The Covenant Service* was adopted by Wesley in 1755 as "a means of increasing serious religion." It is an occasion for believers to join "in a *covenant* to serve God with all our heart and with all our soul" (*A Short History of the People Called Methodists,* 1781). Wesley rejoiced at the blessings people received at these services as they remembered God's grace and renewed their covenant with God and one another. The Covenant Service has often been used around the New Year, but it is appropriate for other times as well. A Covenant Renewal Service, based on Wesley's order, is found in *The United Methodist Book of Worship* (page 288). One of its most important moments occurs when we pray:

> Lord, make me what you will.
> I put myself fully into your hands:
> put me to doing, put me to suffering,
> let me be employed for you, or laid aside for you,
> let me be full, let me be empty,
> let me have all things, let me have nothing.
> I freely and with a willing heart
> give it all to your pleasure and disposal.
> (See also the Covenant hymn and prayer,
> *The United Methodist Hymnal,* 606 and 607)

Avoiding Evil

It was obvious to Wesley that the "means of grace" described above were disciplines given by God by which the Christian life is blessed and strengthened in holiness. All of them are mentioned in the General Rules for the societies. Two others are significant: avoiding evil and doing good. We will examine the importance of doing good in the next chapter when we describe Wesley's concept of "works of mercy." We need to say more here about his advice that by God's grace we must discipline ourselves to avoid evil so that God's blessing may be more deeply implanted in our lives.

A few of the specific admonitions to avoid evil in the General Rules have to do with social relationships. For example, Methodists were not to engage in the buying or selling of slaves, quarreling and fighting with their neighbors, and "Doing to others as we would not they should do unto us." Most of the expectations, however, affect the cultivation of what might be considered personal (as opposed to social) habits of holiness. They included not taking God's name in vain (*Deuteronomy 5:11*), not violating the sabbath (*Deuteronomy 5:12-14*), and not laying up "treasure upon earth" (*Matthew 6:19-21*). Perhaps two illustrations from the General Rules that Wesley amplified in his sermons will help us better understand his devotion to discipline.

Wesley warns against "softness and needless self-indulgence," which were to be resisted at every turn. Wesley believed that the Christian life demands not just temperance but also self-denial and sacrifice. We cannot give in to habits that move God from the center of our lives and damage our spiritual and physical welfare. One of his sermons, "On Redeeming the Time" (1782), deals entirely with sleep in a way that today might seem amusing. We should take all the sleep we need, Wesley stated, and no more. Healthy people need no more than seven hours in a day. If you spend an hour a day in bed more than you need, you have wasted time you could have used more profitably and you have "hurt your health." You have surrendered to "softness and needless self-indulgence." He warned that lying in bed too long between warm sheets (he called it "soaking") makes the flesh "soft and flabby." So much for those wonderful mornings we all cherish when we snatch an extra hour's sleep from the exhausting chores and tasks of modern busy lives! Even with this eccentric wisdom, however, which some of us find difficult to accept, Wesley was simply reminding us of one important truth: we are all stewards of the time God gives us, and we must use it prudently.

A second illustration was Wesley's counsel to avoid the "putting on of gold and costly apparel." In his sermon titled "On Dress" (1786), he charged his followers to be neat and clean. He repeated a saying we have often heard (which actually comes from another author, Rabbi Phinehas ben-Yair): "Cleanliness is indeed next to godliness."

In addition to personal hygiene, Wesley was most concerned that Methodists dress modestly and inexpensively. He gave several reasons for this instruction. Expensive clothing encourages pride and vanity, causing people to think themselves better than others simply because

they dress more elegantly. This must not be the attitude of the fol-
lower of Christ, who is to be humble before God and others. But
above any other objection, Wesley believed that jewelry and costly
clothing injured the ministry to the poor. He bluntly stated:

> Nothing can be more evident than this: for the more you lay out on
> your own apparel, the less you have left to clothe the naked, to feed the
> hungry, to lodge the strangers, to relieve those that are sick and in
> prison, and to lessen the numberless afflictions to which we are exposed
> in this vale of tears.

> When you are laying out that money in costly apparel which you could
> have otherwise spared for the poor, you thereby deprive them of what
> God, the Proprietor of all, had lodged in your hands for their use. If so,
> what you put upon yourself you are, in effect, tearing from the back of
> the naked; as the costly and delicate food which you eat you are snatch-
> ing from the mouth of the hungry.
>
> (Sermon, "On Dress," 1786)

"Let me see, before I die," said Wesley cynically, "a Methodist congregation full as plainly dressed as a Quaker congregation."

Conclusion

Several conclusions can be drawn from this discussion of Wesley's
views on spiritual formation. First, the Christian life requires God's
sustaining grace. We cannot grow in holiness of heart and life without God's forgiveness in Christ and the presence of the Holy Spirit.
Second, God not only promises such supporting grace but actually
provides the means by which it is available to us. These means of
grace are to be employed in a disciplined manner. Third, the means
of grace are not only to be used in a personal way but are also to be
practiced in company with others. Fellowship with others in worship,
prayer, study, and ministry undergirds our identity as Christ's people
and our commitment to serving him. Finally, "works of piety," the disciplined use of the means of grace, will fit us for, and inevitably lead
us to, "works of mercy," mission and ministry to others in the name
of Christ. They equip us to know and experience the true end of religion: total love of God and of neighbor.

Some Questions for Reflection and Discussion

1. Why is the Bible important to you? What is your plan or method for reading and studying the Bible?

2. Have you ever fasted as a spiritual discipline? Why did you fast? How can your sense of the presence of God be strengthened by fasting?

3. What does the Lord's Supper mean to you? How do you feel about John Wesley's recommendation that it is the duty of every Christian to receive the Lord's Supper frequently?

4. How do you feel about Wesley's conviction that we cannot be Christians in solitude? What does it mean to you to share your Christian journey with others?

5. Have you ever participated in a Love Feast or Covenant Renewal Service? What was it like?

"WORKS OF MERCY"

The Practice of the Holy Life and the Transformation of Society

John Wesley frequently defined the essence of Christianity in his writings. It was nothing more than love:

> loving God with all our heart and soul and strength, as having first loved us, as the fountain of all the good we have received, and of all we ever hope to enjoy; and the loving of every soul which God hath made, every [person] on earth, as our own soul. This love we believe to be the medicine of life, the never-failing remedy for all the evils of a disordered world, for all the miseries and vices of [the human race]. . . . This religion we long to see established in the world, a religion of love, and joy, and peace; having its seat in the heart, in the inmost soul, but ever showing itself by its fruits, continually springing forth, not only in all innocence—for love worketh no ill to [our] neighbor—but likewise in every kind of beneficence, spreading virtue and happiness all around it.
>
> (Sermon, "On Laying the Foundation of a New Chapel," 1777)

Genuine inward holiness must show itself in outward holiness. "Works of piety" were worthless without "works of mercy." Faith without works of love, Wesley stated, is the "grand pest of Christianity" (see *James 2:14-26*). Today we might express it this way: "If you want to talk the talk, you have to walk the walk." Talking about our faith isn't enough. It must manifest itself in our dealings with others. It must be a faith filled with the energy of love (*Galatians 5:6*). It is our duty and our privilege to "do good" to others, to engage in "works of mercy." The works are

> . . . feeding the hungry, . . . clothing the naked, . . . entertaining or assisting the stranger, . . . visiting those that are sick or in prison, . . .

comforting the afflicted, . . . instructing the ignorant, . . . reproving the wicked, . . . exhorting and encouraging the well-doer; and if there be any other work of mercy, it is equally included in this direction.
(Sermon, "Upon Our Lord's Sermon on the Mount, VI," 1748)

We have already seen in our discussion of "works of piety" that Wesley preached what he himself practiced. That was equally the case with his views on "works of mercy." He was not content merely to talk about "works of mercy" or to encourage others to do them. He set the pace for the Methodist people. We will see that no one, not the least of persons, was beyond his caring concern. Our purpose in this chapter is to explore some of Wesley's views on "works of mercy" and the manner in which he pioneered the way for Methodism. We cannot specify every instance of his exemplary mission work, but we can highlight a few important areas of ministry.

Money and the Poor

Nothing troubled Wesley more than the misuse of money and the accumulation of wealth. In his sermons and other writings he repeatedly warned that wealth was "the snare of the devil." His study of history convinced him that "riches have in all ages been the bane of genuine Christianity." Whole sermons were devoted to his reservations about wealth, such as "The Danger of Riches" (1781), "On Riches" (1788), and "The Danger of Increasing Riches" (1790).

Wesley believed wealth was a hindrance to holiness, offering plain reasons why: at the very least, wealth discourages love of God because it encourages the love of possessions. At worst, it promotes idolatry by replacing God with money and property. Those who love money cannot love God (*Matthew 6:24*). Wealth also discourages love of neighbor, tempting us to exploit our neighbors for the sake of maintaining and increasing our riches. Those who love money cannot love their neighbors. For Wesley true holiness, the complete, unconditional love of God and neighbor, is threatened by the accumulation of wealth.

Never content merely to offer criticism and warning, Wesley gave advice in his sermon "The Use of Money" (1760). He made three simple suggestions. First, "Gain all you can." There is nothing wrong with earning money, provided we make it by honest labor, without harming our minds or bodies through overwork, and as long as we do not exploit or hurt our neighbors by our gain. Christians must use the talents God gives to earn their living.

Second, "Save all you can." Since everything in life comes from God, including the ability to make money, we must receive God's blessings thankfully and act as good stewards of God's gift. Wesley believed that Christ's people should live plainly without wasting God's gifts. They should cut off every expense that is unnecessary and "serves only to indulge foolish desire." They should spend nothing that does not please and glorify God.

Third, "Give all you can" (*Acts 20:35*). This is the culmination of his counsel. You must provide the essentials for yourself and your family: food, clothing, shelter, and the other necessities for preserving health and strength. When these have been furnished, the surplus must be used to assist those in need, especially the poor, in the church and in the rest of the world. Hoard nothing, he urged. Share what you have with those who are in want. Sharing with them is a concrete sign of giving all to God. As the Methodist movement matured, Wesley was afraid that his people, having worked hard and lived frugally, would grow wealthy and abandon their commitment to the poor. Indeed, as they became more prosperous, he felt it was necessary to remind them continually to give to others all they could.

Poverty was widespread in eighteenth-century England, especially in the cities. One of the great contrasts of the time was the gulf between those who had much more than they needed and the absolutely destitute. Both John and Charles Wesley were greatly concerned about the poor and exhibited great compassion toward them. Charles's commitment to the poor is expressed in a prayerful hymn:

> Thy mind throughout my life be shown,
>   While listening to the sufferer's cry,
> The widow's and the orphan's groan,
>   On mercy's wings I swiftly fly,
> The poor and helpless to relieve,
>   My life, my all, for them to give.

As usual, John not only talked about the ills of poverty but also acted personally to relieve the plight of the poor. He urged

Methodists to do the same. He went among poor people to declare God's love for them in Christ. They, too, were people for whom Christ died. He aimed to give them a new sense of self-worth. Wesley ate with the poor. He slept with the poor. He leased houses for homeless widows and children. He gave away most of the money that passed through his hands. Some of his contemporaries claimed that he was the most charitable person in England, whose generosity toward the poor knew no bounds. The Methodist people followed his example. Collections of cash, food, and clothing in the societies and classes were used to ease the pain of poverty. We will note further evidence of Wesley's mission to the poor in the rest of this chapter.

Health, Medicine, and the Sick

Wesley was concerned about the spiritual welfare of people but was also keenly interested in their physical well-being. He displayed a special compassion for the sick. One of his sermons is titled "On Visiting the Sick" (1786). When he learned that many of the sick in the London society were neglected because the leaders of their society did not have time to minister to their needs, he organized "Visitors of the Sick" to tend them (*Matthew 25:31-46*). He chose forty-six men and women to do this work, dividing the city into twenty-three districts and assigning two visitors to each district to visit those who were ill. He provided guidelines for the "Visitors." They were to visit every person in their district three times a week, to inquire about the person's spiritual and physical welfare and to offer or secure advice for them. Visitors were directed "to do anything for them" that they could.

Wesley was persuaded that women, following the pattern of the deaconess in the early church, were especially gifted to engage in this ministry. His comments about their role as visitors of the sick also reveal something basic about his great respect for their standing before God and their participation in the ministry to which all Christians are called. He wrote:

> But may not women as well as men bear a part in this honourable service? Undoubtedly they may; nay, they ought—it is meet, right, and their bounden duty. Herein there is no difference: "there is neither male nor female in Christ Jesus" [Galatians 3:28]. Indeed it has long passed for a

maxim with many that "women are only to be seen, not heard." And accordingly many of them are brought up in such a manner as if they were only designed for agreeable playthings! But is this doing honour to the sex? Or is it a real kindness to them? No; it is the deepest unkindness; it is horrid cruelty; it is mere . . . barbarity. And I know not how any woman of sense and spirit can submit to it. Let all you that have it in your power assert the right which the God of nature has given you. Yield not to that vile bondage any longer. You, as well as men, are rational creatures. You, like them, were made in the image of God; you are equally creatures for immortality. You too are called of God, as you have time, to "do good unto all. . . ." Be "not disobedient to the heavenly calling." Whenever you have opportunity, do all the good you can, particularly to your poor sick neighbour. And every one of you likewise "shall receive your own reward according to your own labour."

(Sermon, "On Visiting the Sick," 1786)

Wesley was not content simply to provide visitors for the sick. For most of his life he was also intensely interested in preventing and curing disease (see *Acts 3:1-10*). His reading included books about health and medicine. His journal and letters contain frequent references to matters related to the physical welfare of his readers, including the medicinal uses of electricity.

The best-known indication of his interest in health and medicine was his 1747 publication *Primitive Physick; or An Easy and Natural Method of Curing Most Diseases*. This book of advice on health and cures was directed especially at those who had no access to medical care because of poverty or lack of a physician nearby. The book was reprinted many times during Wesley's lifetime. Two parts of it are particularly interesting to us.

First, Wesley offers his suggestions for maintaining good health, prescribing an eighteenth-century plan that in some respects sounds remarkably modern. He recommends a program of fresh air, diet, sleep, and exercise. Since the "air we breathe is of great consequence to our health," we should breathe clean fresh air outdoors whenever possible. Diet should consist of "plain" (not highly seasoned) food, including plenty of vegetables and a modest amount of meat. Water is the "wholesomest" beverage, he advises. Suppers should be light and eaten at least two or three hours before bedtime. We should go to bed about 9:00 P.M and rise at 4:00 or 5:00 A.M.

Exercise, he writes, "is indispensably necessary to health and long life." For those who can do it, walking is best. Fearing the ill effects of inactivity on students and office workers, Wesley recommends that "those who read or write much should learn to do it standing [if they are able]; otherwise it will impair their health." Exercise should always be taken on an empty stomach. It should never be overdone to the point of weariness, and after exercise we should cool down "by degrees." He also warns against yielding to sudden overpowering emotions, such as revenge and anger, that have a tendency to cause acute diseases.

Second, Wesley's *Primitive Physick* also prescribes remedies for common injuries and illnesses. He notes that he had tried many of them himself. Some of the remedies seem rather contemporary. For example, "To prevent Swelling from a Bruise. Immediately apply a cloth, five or six times doubled, dipt in cold water, and new dipt when it grows warm." Others, however, are humorous. For a head cold Wesley advises, "Pare very thin the yellow rind of an orange. Roll it up inside out, and thrust a roll into each nostril." Nowadays we prefer our Vitamin C tablets.

For a brief time Wesley actually dispensed medicine from his chapels in London, Bristol, and Newcastle. Several hundred people received assistance from these free clinics (*A Plain Account of the People Called Methodists*, 1749). Some criticized Wesley for his amateur dabbling in healing and medicine, but he was persuaded that he supplied advice and care for many who otherwise would not have had any.

Wesley understood both the health and social issues related to the intemperate use of alcoholic beverages, especially liquors such as gin and brandy. He described distilled liquor as a "certain, though slow, poison," "liquid fire," prepared by the devil and his angels. Although he allowed for the use of liquor for "medicinal purposes," he cautioned against its consumption as a regular beverage and condemned those who sold it as "poisoners." About the "sellers of spirits" he stressed: "They murder His Majesty's subjects by wholesale, neither does their eye pity or spare [them]. They drive [their customers] to hell like sheep." Alcohol was not only a threat to good health, it was a menace to morality. Drunkenness affected the family and community, causing chaos in both. Wesley laid foundations for Methodism's traditional call to abstain from beverage alcohol and its warnings about the use of drugs (see United Methodism's Social Principles in *The Book of Discipline*).

Prisons and Prisoners

"Acts of mercy," love of neighbor and doing good, included reaching out to all people regardless of their circumstances. People in the most dishonorable and wretched circumstances needed to hear the gospel of God's forgiveness and to experience God's care through the ministry of others. The Wesleys and their followers were determined to carry their mission to prisons and prisoners, whom many in England believed undeserving of any compassion (*Matthew 25:31-46*).

The English legal system in the eighteenth century was harsh. The laws were strict, especially regarding debtors and crimes against property. Punishment of the poor was particularly severe, while crimes against the poor were often considered trivial. Prisoners were often held for long periods in filthy, unsanitary prisons awaiting their trials. They were regularly mistreated by their keepers. Legal punishment could include long periods of confinement; whippings; brandings; transportation to distant colonies; and, in many cases, death by hanging. The death penalty applied to a wide variety of offenses, some of which we would consider minor, such as poaching, theft of clothing or small amounts of money, or stealing cattle or sheep.

The Wesleys began their work among prisoners in their Oxford University days and continued it throughout their ministries, especially in London and Bristol. They visited prisoners, preached and read the Bible to them, prayed with them, and provided food and clothing for them. John and Charles enlisted Methodist people to assist them with this work. Methodists helped prisoners maintain ties with family and friends. They even rode the carts to the gallows with those who were to be hanged, singing and praying.

On November 13, 1748, John Wesley noted in his journal the death of Sarah Peters, one of his faithful Methodist followers. She was a visitor to prisoners at the infamous Newgate Prison in London. Wesley mentioned that Peters called on John Lancaster, a wayward Methodist who had been affiliated with the Foundry Chapel in London. Lancaster had stolen property from the chapel and had been arrested, tried, and condemned to death. Believing that Lancaster did not deserve death for his crime, Peters spared no energy in seeking a pardon for him. Her efforts to have him freed were unsuccessful. Her ministry to Lancaster, however, was undaunted. Wesley noted:

> she went constantly to Newgate, sometimes alone, sometimes with one or two others, visited [Lancaster and] all that were condemned to death in their cells, exhorted them, prayed with them, and had the comfort of finding them, every time more athirst for God than before; and of being followed, whenever she went away, with abundance of prayers and blessings.
>
> *(Journal, November 13, 1748)*

Peters visited the prison even though a severe outbreak of dangerously contagious fever raged throughout the facility. Her testimony was successful. She witnessed a change in Lancaster and others facing the gallows and rejoiced as they experienced God's comforting and strengthening presence. On November 3, a few days after Lancaster's hanging, Peters became gravely ill, probably from the jail fever. Ten days later she was dead: her Newgate ministry had cost Sarah her life. Wesley's moving and grateful tribute to her ministry ends with his observation that through all her suffering she had kept the faith and at last "her spirit . . . returned to God."

Wesley grieved over the inhumane conditions of the prisons he visited. He lamented the unequal standards of justice and legal treatment between the wealthy and the poor. Without fail, he displayed a keen regard for the prisoner to whom he offered the grace of Christ in word and deed. (See, for example, *Prayers for Condemned Malefactors,* 1785.) His concern for the prisoner, the prison conditions, and the criminal justice system laid the groundwork for United Methodism's present positions on these matters, which are found in the Social Principles and *The Book of Resolutions.*

Slavery

John Wesley first encountered the enslavement of Africans while he was a missionary in America. His initial contact with slaves in South Carolina led to opportunities to provide Christian instruction for them. He was so pleased with his success in sharing the gospel with a few of them that he conceived a plan to reach a larger number:

Perhaps one of the easiest and shortest ways to instruct the American Negroes in Christianity would be first to inquire after and find out some of the most serious of the planters. Then, having inquired of them which of their slaves were best inclined, and understood English, to go to them from plantation to plantation, staying as long as appeared necessary at each.

(Journal, April 27, 1737)

There is no evidence to show that Wesley ever put this plan into effect, but it is clear that throughout his ministry he was always willing to preach to people and to teach them regardless of their race.

The African slave trade was the target of his strongest rebuke. Wesley described it as the "execrable sum of all villainies." Wesley despised all forms of slavery as inhuman and contrary to the will of God. Nothing excused the exploitation of one person or group by another. Every person deserved to be treated as someone created by God for whom Christ died (*Isaiah 61:1-2; Luke 4:18-19*). In 1774, he published *Thoughts Upon Slavery*, in which he condemned American slavery and England's involvement in it, pleading for its abolition. It is important to follow Wesley's argument against slavery.

First, in answer to the claim that African homelands were "horrid, dreary, and barren," and that it was to their benefit that Africans were taken to America, Wesley argued that Africa was beautiful, fruitful, and pleasant. Second, the people of Africa were not "stupid, senseless, brutish, lazy barbarians, . . . fierce, cruel, perfidious savages," as some alleged. On the contrary, they were industrious, quiet, orderly, civil, kind, religious, ready to help those in need, just, honest, and of good disposition. Unless, Wesley added scornfully, "white men have taught them to be otherwise."

Wesley found the purchase, transportation, and treatment of African slaves scandalous. They were fraudently lured, forced, or sold into slavery only for financial gain. The manner of their transport was brutal. The hundreds of men, women, and children crowded into each slave ship suffered heat, thirst, hunger, and disease. Not only did many die on the ships, it was a wonder any survived. After their arrival in America, they were sold apart from family or friends, then poorly fed, scarcely clothed, forced into hard labor for long hours, and whipped and tortured if they did not perform up to expectation or attempted to escape.

Banished from their country, from their friends and relations forever, from every comfort of life, they are reduced to a state scarce anyway preferable to that of beasts of burden. . . . Did the creator intend that the noblest creatures in the visible world should live such a life as this?

(*Thoughts Upon Slavery*, 1774)

Try as they might, Wesley argued, no one could defend the slave trade. Many said that slavery was an economic necessity. It was essential in order to cultivate the land and to enhance the nation's wealth. Wesley replied that under such circumstances it was better if the land remained uncultivated, adding:

Wealth is not necessary to the glory of any nation; but wisdom, virtue, justice, mercy, generosity, public spirit, love of our country. These are necessary to the real glory of a nation; but abundance of wealth is not. . . . Better no trade than trade procured by villainy. It is far better to have no wealth, than to gain wealth at the expense of virtue. Better is honest poverty, than all the riches bought by the tears, and sweat, and blood of our fellow-creatures.

(*Thoughts Upon Slavery*, 1774)

Thoughts Upon Slavery ended with pleas to the captains of slave ships, merchants in the slave trade, and owners of slaves to abolish slavery altogether. Wesley announced God's judgment and punishment of those who persisted in this "villainy." He also appealed to their sense of justice, kindness, and mercy, urging:

Give liberty to whom liberty is due, that is, to every [human] child . . . to every partaker of human nature. Let none serve you but by his own act and deed, by his own voluntary choice. Away with all whips, all chains, all compulsion! Be gentle toward all . . . ; and see that you invariably do unto every one as you would he should do unto you.

(*Thoughts Upon Slavery*, 1774)

The publication of his attack on the profitable slave trade was risky for Wesley and the Methodist people who were identified with his views. His opinions were unacceptable to anyone who profited from slavery and were also an affront to those who considered the Africans their inferiors. For the latter group Wesley had further unsettling words: "The inhabitants of Africa . . . are not inferior to the inhabitants of Europe; to some of them they are greatly superior."

Education

We have already noticed that Wesley valued the mind as one of God's most precious gifts to us. He believed that reason is important, not only in the routine business of life but also in religion. Of course, the two could not be separated in the life of a Christian. It is not surprising, therefore, that we find Wesley promoting educational enterprises to make his people more knowledgeable and his preachers more effective. He did everything he could to encourage people to learn, not only about religion and theology but also the basic skills they needed to function in their daily lives. Three illustrations will help us understand the importance he attached to education.

1. He published books, pamphlets, and magazines. It should be obvious now that Wesley used the printing press to great advantage. He wrote or edited hundreds of publications, ranging from one-page news sheets to the fifty-volume *Christian Library*. Although most of these dealt with religion and theology, he also published books on poetry, philosophy, geography, science, and biography. His purpose was to put into the hands of Methodists and others inexpensive books and pamphlets to enrich their understanding of the Christian faith and to extend their knowledge of the world in which they lived. In some cases the publications were made available free to those who could not pay for them.

Wesley was devoted to reading good literature and considered it his duty to help others do the same. In 1778, Wesley began to publish the monthly *Arminian Magazine*,* a periodical for Methodists that provided inspirational poetry and testimonies and discussions on theological issues. The United Methodist Publishing House and other agencies keep alive today the tradition of communicating by the printed word begun by John Wesley.

2. He founded schools. There were many schools in eighteenth-century England, including charity schools for poor children. However, Wesley observed that there were too many children and adults, especially among the poor, who had never been enrolled in any educational program. He therefore set about to establish schools for them. He started a school at the Foundry in London to train the chil-

dren of the poor and to provide a better education for children who were enrolled in schools that did not offer them sufficient moral guidance (*Proverbs 22:6*). Schools were also begun in Bristol, Newcastle, and in other places where there was a significant Methodist presence.

One of Wesley's most impressive educational ventures was the new Kingswood School that he opened in 1748 in a mining village near Bristol. Its purpose was "with God's assistance, to train up children, in every branch of useful learning" (*A Short Account of the School in Kingswood, Near Bristol*, 1768). Wesley enthusiastically maintained that students who completed its course of study would be better scholars than most of the graduates of the universities at Oxford and Cambridge. The curriculum included courses on reading, writing, mathematics, languages (Latin, Greek, Hebrew, French), history, philosophy, geography, science, literature, music, and theology. In true Wesleyan fashion the school had a rigorous set of rules that the children were required to obey. The students' daily schedule began with rising at 4:00 A.M. and concluded with bedtime at 8:00 P.M. Wesley even prescribed each day's food menu. Fridays were observed as fast days until 3:00 P.M. for the "healthy." The Sunday schedule was slightly more relaxed but still required attendance at three worship services, learning hymns or poems, and private instruction. Play was not allowed at any time since, as the rules stated: "He that plays when he is a child, will play when he is a man."

By modern standards Wesley's educational philosophy is severe. Its relentless schedule allowed children little time to enjoy their childhood. It is typical of Wesley's belief, however, that education must be pursued earnestly and methodically if the child is to be fitted for a useful, moral, and religious life. A stanza of Charles Wesley's hymn written for the 1748 opening of Kingswood gives voice to the Wesleys' vision for the school:

> Unite the two so long disjoined,
>   Knowledge and vital piety:
> Learning and holiness combined,
>   And truth and love, let all men see
> In those whom up to thee we give,
>   Thine, wholly thine, to die and live.

Since Wesley's day, Methodists have established educational institutions in various parts of the world—secondary schools, colleges and universities, and theological seminaries. They are much different from the Kingswood model but retain commitment to the cultivation of the mind as a sign of Christian stewardship.

Ewha Woman's University in Seoul, Korea, is one example of the church's dedication to Wesley's educational vision. Begun in 1886 as a class in the home of Mary F. Scranton, a missionary of the Woman's Foreign Missionary Society of the Methodist Episcopal Church, its purpose has been to change society through the education of Korean women. Ewha remains one of the largest and most influential universities in the world.

3. John Wesley supported Sunday schools (Letter to Charles Atmore, March 24, 1790) but was not the founder of the Sunday school. That honor is usually reserved for Robert Raikes, a newspaper publisher in Gloucester, England, who started a Sunday school in 1780 for children of local poor families. The first Methodist Sunday school was begun earlier, organized in 1769 by Hannah Ball, a Methodist laywoman, in High Wycombe, a town between Oxford and London. Wesley saw great promise in Sunday schools as a means of "reviving religion throughout the nation" and supported them for their potential to deepen religious experience and discipleship. Methodists around the world have found the Sunday school an important educational component in the church's ministry. In many places recently, however, the Sunday school has fallen on difficult times with enrollment and attendance plummeting.

War

John Wesley detested war. He asked, "Who can reconcile war, I will not say to religion [only], but to any degree of reason or common sense?" He continued,

> [People] in general can never be [considered] to be reasonable creatures, till they know not war any more. So long as this monster stalks uncontrolled, where is reason, virtue, humanity? They are utterly excluded; they have no place; they are a name, and nothing more.
> *(The Doctrine of Original Sin, 1756)*

69

According to Wesley there are "innumerable" causes of war. Chief among them is the greedy ambition of nations and their leaders to extend their territory and possessions. Wesley cynically wrote:

> Sometimes our neighbours want the things which we have, or have the things we want: So both fight, until they take ours, or we take theirs. It is a reason for invading a country, if the people have been wasted by famine, destroyed by pestilence, or embroiled by faction; or to attack our nearest ally, if part of [their] land would make our dominions more round and compact. . . .
>
> Another cause for making war is this: A crew are driven by storm they know not where: at length they make the land and go ashore; they are entertained with kindness. They give the country a new name; set up a stone or rotten plank for a memorial; murder a dozen of the natives, and bring away a couple by force. Here commences a new right of dominion: Ships are sent, and the natives driven out or destroyed. And this [it is claimed] is done to civilize and convert a barbarous and idolatrous people.
>
> (*The Doctrine of Original Sin*, 1756)

There is no plainer proof of the depravity of individuals and the "degeneracy" of nations than their pursuit of war. Such acts of violence clearly show the universal seriousness of sin.

Christians are called to do everything possible to avert war and to promote peace, Wesley believed (see *Isaiah 2:4*). When the revolution of the American colonies against England looked imminent, Wesley advised Thomas Rankin, his chief assistant in America, and his American preachers:

> It is your part to be peace-makers, to be loving and tender to all, but to addict yourselves to no party. In spite of all solicitations, of rough or smooth words, say not one word against one side or the other side. Keep yourselves pure, do all you can to help and soften all.
>
> (Letter, March 1, 1775)

Although Wesley deeply desired to see the antagonism between England and the American colonies settled peacefully, when war between them began, his intense loyalty to King George III and his country led him to support England's side.

Wesley was not a pacifist; he never denied that war might have to be an instrument of national policy, especially in self-defense or to preserve order. War, however, was never preferable in the settlement of any dispute. "The duty of the Christian is to extend 'loving arms of faith and prayer' around one's contentious brethren." A hymn of Charles Wesley's expresses the demonic nature of war and the desire for peace:

> Our earth we now lament to see
>   with floods of wickedness overflowed;
> with violence, wrong, and cruelty,
>   one wide-extended field of blood,
> where men like fiends each other tear,
>   in all the hellish rage of war.
>
> As listed on Abaddon's side,
>   they mangle their own flesh, and slay;
> Tophet is moved, and opens wide
>   its mouth for its enormous prey;
> and myriads sink beneath the grave,
>   and plunge into the flaming wave.
>
> O might the universal Friend
>   this havoc of his creatures see!
> Bid our unnatural discord end;
>   declare us reconciled in thee!
> Write kindness in our inward parts
>   and chase the murderer from our hearts!
>
> Who now against each other rise,
>   the nations of the earth constrain
> to follow after peace, and prize
>   the blessings of thy righteous reign,
> the joys of unity to prove,
>   the paradise of perfect love!
>   ("Our Earth We Now Lament to See,"
>   *The United Methodist Hymnal*, 449)

[*Abaddon* is a Hebrew name that means "ruler of the place of death and destruction." *Tophet* is the Hebrew name for a place south of ancient Jerusalem where pagan sacrifices of children were offered to the gods, a practice criticized by Isaiah and Jeremiah.]

Conclusion

We are now in a position to draw some conclusions from our discussion of Wesley's views on "works of mercy." First, Wesley believed that "works of piety" and "works of mercy" are inseparable companions in the genuine Christian life. Authentic personal holiness is also social holiness. Bible study, prayer, fasting, Christian conversation, the Lord's Supper, public worship, and the other disciplines of the Christian life are critical to the holy life; but holy living is impossible until Christians engage in "doing good" to their neighbors. In word and deed, faith must be active in love. God's grace prepares us, accepts us, and sustains us. But then God's grace expects something of us: our faithful discipleship and ministry in Christ's name, undergirded by the presence and power of the Holy Spirit.

Second, Wesley not only preached and wrote about the necessity of "works of mercy," he also lived them out in his own ministry. He did not expect Methodists to do what he was unwilling to do himself. He preached what he practiced. This is always a major challenge of the Christian life: by the grace of God to bring our words and acts into conformity with what we say we believe and what we know to be right. Wesley was never content to talk about changes that were needed in eighteenth-century England: he was committed to working for them.

Third, Wesley believed that the best means of transforming society was the change God worked in the individual. This is important, but often something more systematic is necessary to bring about social change. We all pray that individuals will be so converted by grace that they will be committed to avoid evil and to do good to their neighbors, resulting in social reformation. However, just and righteous social transformation often must be actively sought by additional means. For example, Wesley pleaded with slave ship captains, slave traders, and slave owners to give up their villainous involvement in slavery; but he did not actively and directly pursue political means with the King and Parliament to end it. While he urgently begged individuals to change, the slave trade continued.

We must add, however, that while Wesley did not directly approach the government to outlaw slavery, his views strongly influenced and encouraged some of the most effective leaders in the anti-slavery movement. One was William Wilberforce, who was a member of

Parliament. Parliament finally outlawed England's participation in the slave trade in 1807. Christians today must not only look to individuals to change but must also search for other appropriate means to bring about social transformation.

We turn next to the ways in which Wesley's theology, his views on "works of piety," and his emphasis on "works of mercy" were implemented among his people in North America.

Some Questions for Reflection and Discussion

1. What do you think about Wesley's advice on the use of money: "Gain all you can. Save all you can. Give all you can"? What are the practical implications of each of these in your personal life and in the life of the church?

2. Given Wesley's concern about people's physical health, what should we do about our own health? By what means can we demonstrate our concern about the health and welfare of others?

3. What do you know about persons in prison? In what sort of conditions should they live? Does your church participate in a prison ministry?

4. John Wesley was deeply concerned about education. In the Social Principles of The United Methodist Church printed in *The Book of Discipline*, there is a statement on education in the section titled "The Political Community." What does it call us to do?

5. The Social Principles, in the section titled "The World Community," say, "We believe war is incompatible with the teachings and example of Christ." Read the whole paragraph. How does the church carry out this official statement?

5
CHAPTER

WESLEY'S PEOPLE
IN NORTH AMERICA

In 1768, John Wesley received a letter from Thomas Taylor, a Methodist layperson in New York. Taylor begged Wesley to send an "able, experienced preacher" to work with the growing number of Methodists in the city. They needed a person "of wisdom, and a good disciplinarian," Taylor stated, "one whose heart and soul are in the work." He continued, "With respect to the money for the payment of a preacher's passage over, if [no one else] could procure it, we would sell our coats and shirts and pay it." It would take several months before Wesley could find volunteers in England to send to America.

Methodism began in America just a few years before Taylor's letter to Wesley. It was organized by laypeople who were devoted to the gospel Wesley preached and who had been members of his societies in Ireland and England. One of them, Robert Strawbridge, a native of Ireland, made the long voyage across the Atlantic and settled with his wife, Elizabeth, in Frederick County, Maryland, around 1760. Strawbridge had been a Methodist lay preacher and continued his preaching shortly after arriving in the colonies. He organized Methodist societies in Maryland and Virginia and was responsible for constructing the first Methodist meetinghouse in America. Elizabeth's witness led to John Evans' embracing the Christian faith; Evans is believed to be the first Methodist convert in America.

In 1766, two more Irish Methodists who were cousins, Philip Embury and Barbara Heck, formed a Methodist class in New York City. Like Strawbridge, Embury had been a Methodist lay preacher in Ireland; but it was Heck's prodding that convinced him that he needed to take up the work in their new land. The Methodist presence in New York grew from a small class meeting into a thriving society and ultimately became the John Street United Methodist Church, a congregation that continues its ministry today in lower Manhattan.

A British army officer, Captain Thomas Webb, who was an active

Methodist when he resided in Bristol, England, became another of the earliest founders of American Methodism. Webb assisted in establishing the work in New York. He was also committed to the spread of the Methodist message to other communities; and, in 1767, he organized the first Methodist group in Philadelphia. The ministry of the Philadelphia society continues today as St. George's United Methodist Church. From these three modest beginnings in Maryland, New York, and Philadelphia, Methodism took root in the American colonies.

In 1769, Wesley was able to fulfill Thomas Taylor's request to send lay preachers to America. Richard Boardman and Joseph Pilmore volunteered for the mission. Two years later two more preachers were dispatched, Richard Wright and Francis Asbury. Asbury became the most influential leader in early American Methodism. In 1773, Wesley sent two more preachers, Thomas Rankin and George Shadford. Shortly after his arrival, Rankin called the first annual conference of Methodist preachers in America. They met in Philadelphia.

The lay preachers sent by Wesley and those who were already resident in America, like the Strawbridges, were deeply devoted to preaching the Methodist message of salvation and holy living. They were responsible not only for sustaining the Methodist work that already existed but also for extending its presence wherever new societies and classes could be started. Under their leadership the numbers of Methodists grew steadily.

From the beginning American Methodism included both white and African American members. Among those present at one of the earliest Methodist meetings in America, organized by Embury and Heck in New York in 1766, was an African American servant named Betty. Other African Americans were attracted to New York Methodism and were among the contributors to the building of its first meetinghouse. They became active participants in worship and witness in many other places. By 1795, when the membership of American Methodism numbered about 60,000, more than one in five (12,170) were African American.

Women were important members of the early societies and classes. Mary Thorne of Philadelphia became the first of many women who served as class leaders in American Methodism. Catharine Livingston Garrettson, married to one of the earliest American Methodist preachers, was well known for her devotion to the Christian faith and her loyalty to Methodism. She organized prayer groups, taught the Bible to children and adults, and acted as a spiritual mentor for a wide variety of people. She was typical of many women associated with the Wesleyan movement in her unstinting support of its preachers and laypeople, her deep spirituality, and her commitment to Methodism's expansion.

The Revolutionary War created a major crisis for Methodists in America. Wesley's pamphlet, *A Calm Address to Our American Colonies*, published in 1775, was critical of the colonists' desire for independence. He felt the colonists owed their complete and unquestioning loyalty to England and should not seek a separation. Americans who favored independence and who became familiar with Wesley's views suspected that his preachers and other followers in America were opposed to their freedom from English rule. Furthermore, as the war began, all the missionary preachers sent by Wesley except Francis Asbury returned to England because they believed that the Revolution was wrong. Asbury stayed because he loved the land and its people, but he refused to take an oath of allegiance to the Revolutionary cause that included an obligation to bear arms.

One of his fellow preachers, Jesse Lee, another outstanding leader of early American Methodism, shared Wesley's distaste for war and refused to fight. Lee did drive a supply wagon for the Revolutionary army, and he later served terms as chaplain in both the United States House of Representatives and Senate.

During and after the Revolution, American Methodists faced further difficulties. Many Anglican* (Church of England) clergy also returned to England or fled to Canada, since they were unsympathetic to the Revolution. Methodists in America, like their sisters and brothers across the Atlantic, were generally members of Anglican parishes. They looked to Anglican clergy, as well as to their own Methodist lay preachers, for spiritual leadership. Since their lay preachers were unordained and therefore unable to administer the sacraments, they were especially dependent on the Anglican priests for the baptism of their children and the administration of the Lord's Supper. Considering how important baptism and the Lord's Supper were to these people, what were they to do if no Anglican clergy were available to provide these means of grace? Some, like Strawbridge, felt that the circumstances called for the Methodist preachers to administer the sacraments, even though they were unordained. Others, like Asbury, felt that it was entirely inappropriate for the unordained Methodist lay preachers to baptize and serve Communion.

Wesley tried to remedy the situation of his American followers by asking Anglican bishops in England to ordain some of his lay preachers for America. When they refused, Wesley was forced to make a radical decision. He was persuaded that in emergencies ordained ministers who were not bishops had the right to ordain others. Therefore in September 1784, assisted by two other Anglican priests, he ordained two of his lay preachers for Methodist work in America.

On September 18, 1784, Wesley sent the newly ordained preachers to America with Thomas Coke, an Anglican priest who was also dedicated to the Methodist movement. Coke and his companions carried with them instructions for organizing an American Methodist church, including the ordination of some of the lay preachers; a prayerbook devised by Wesley based on the liturgy of the Church of England and titled *The Sunday Service of the Methodists in North America*; a short hymnbook titled *A Collection of Psalms and Hymns for the Lord's Day*, which was bound with *The Sunday Service*; and directions that Coke and Francis Asbury were to be the "superintendents" of the newly formed American church.

In December 1784, a conference of the Methodist preachers, now usually called the Christmas Conference, was held at Lovely Lane Chapel in Baltimore, Maryland, to constitute the new church. The preachers adopted a name: the Methodist Episcopal Church in America. Asbury and Coke were unanimously elected "superintendents." (Later they were called "bishops," a title Wesley felt was inappropriate. He wrote: "Men may call me a knave or a fool, a rascal, a scoundrel, and I am content; but they shall never by my consent call me Bishop!")

The preachers adopted a book of discipline that stated the purpose of the new church: "to reform the continent and to spread scriptural holiness through these lands." General Rules and Articles of Religion (drafted by Wesley based on those of the Church of England) were also adopted. Several preachers received ordination from Coke and those ordained by Wesley, thus permitting them to administer the sacraments. The Christmas Conference also approved a motion that prohibited Methodists from engaging in the slave trade. The first Discipline of the Methodist Episcopal Church (1785) affirmed the American Methodists' loyalty to John Wesley and pledged to obey his instructions. It stated: "During the Life of the Rev. Mr. Wesley, we acknowledge ourselves his [children] in the Gospel, ready in matters belonging to Church-Government, to obey his commands."

A Methodist church had been born in America!

Within a few years two other churches were born that had close associations with early American Methodism. Both were started among German-speaking people. One was the Church of the United Brethren in Christ, founded by Philip William Otterbein and Martin Boehm. Otterbein was friendly with Methodists and assisted in Asbury's ordination at the Christmas Conference. The United Brethren preached an evangelical message like the Methodists and adopted a similar order of church government when they organized in 1800.

The other church was the Evangelical Association (later the Evangelical Church) founded by Jacob Albright, a farmer and tile-maker in eastern Pennsylvania. Albright's followers adopted an organizational pattern similar to the Methodists and were influenced by Wesley's theology. They held their first annual conference in 1807. In 1946, the United Brethren and the Evangelicals united to form the Evangelical United Brethren Church.

During several decades following the 1784 Christmas Conference, the Methodist Episcopal Church suffered several serious divisions over issues of racial inclusiveness and slavery, the power and authority of bishops, and the role of laity in the leadership of the church. In 1939, three of these Methodist churches—the Methodist Episcopal Church; the Methodist Protestant Church; and the Methodist Episcopal Church, South—reunited to form The Methodist Church.

In 1968, the Evangelical United Brethren united with The Methodist Church to form The United Methodist Church. In the remainder of this chapter we will pay special attention to the Methodist side of the United Methodist family, since they were more directly influenced by Wesley's views on theology, "works of piety," and "works of mercy."

11-25-02

Theology

Wesley sent theological standards for American Methodism in the *Sunday Service of the Methodists in North America,* the document that Thomas Coke brought with him in 1784. A section of the *Sunday Service* contains "Articles of Religion."* These Articles are Wesley's edited version of the Thirty-nine Articles of the Church of England, the official statement of the theological views of the Anglican Church that had been adopted in 1571. Wesley shortened these to twenty-four Articles. The American preachers added an Article at the Christmas Conference in 1784 that recognized the United States as a "sovereign and independent nation." The Articles of Religion remain in Part II of *The Book of Discipline* titled "Doctrinal Standards and Our Theological Task." They are protected by one of the Restrictive Rules of the Constitution of The United Methodist Church, which reads: "The General Conference shall not revoke, alter, or change our Articles of Religion or establish any new standards or rules of doctrine contrary to our present existing and established standards of doctrine." From Wesley's time to the present, the Articles of Religion have been recognized as an important theological guide for American Methodists and their successors.

The Articles of Religion may be divided into five main groups. The first group (Articles I-IV) state belief in the triune God, "the maker and preserver of all things." They speak of Jesus as the one who reconciles us to God and the Holy Spirit whose presence is a gift to us. The second group (Articles V-VI) speak about the adequacy of Scripture for determining what the Christian is to believe and do. They affirm the importance of the Bible that offers God's plan of everlasting life. The third group (Articles VII-XII) underscore the seriousness of sin, the freedom of the person by God's "preventing" (prevenient) grace, justification (salvation) by faith, the holy life that springs "out of a true and lively faith," and the dangerous possibility of falling away from God.

The fourth group (Articles XIII-XXII) speak about the church and the sacraments. The church is said to be the congregation of faithful people "in which the pure Word of God is preached, and the sacraments duly administered." Baptism and the Lord's Supper, United Methodism's two sacraments, are described as "signs of grace, and

God's good will toward us" by which our faith is confirmed, strengthened, and enlivened. It must be noted that some of the Articles in this group are severely critical of Roman Catholic belief and practice; from today's perspective these appear to be quite outdated. The last group (Articles XXIII-XXV) deal with the relationship and responsibility of the Christian to the government. They also include an important Article that calls for giving liberally to the poor.

The Articles of Religion that Wesley sent to America do not include all the major emphases of his theology that we noted in Chapter 2. There is no mention, for example, of the new birth, or assurance, or Christian perfection. There is no question, however, that Wesley believed they contained theological ideas central to the Christian faith and that they should be employed by his people in America as standards for their understanding of Christianity.

In addition to the Articles of Religion, at least two other writings by Wesley were viewed as central theological standards for American Methodists. These are the sermons that Wesley identified as teaching the essentials of his theology and *The Explanatory Notes Upon the New Testament*. Both works were reprinted several times and were made available to both preachers and lay people from the earliest days of the church in America. The sermons, *The Explanatory Notes Upon the New Testament*, and the Articles of Religion are doctrinal standards, along with The Confession of Faith of the Evangelical United Brethren Church (which did not come directly from Wesley but is in agreement with the main emphases of his theology). All are in *The Book of Discipline of The United Methodist Church.*

Another key document in Part II of *The Book of Discipline* is titled "Our Theological Task."* This section first appeared in the *Discipline* in 1972 and was revised to its present form in 1988. While the document did not originate with Wesley, it represents the first comprehensive statement of what some have called the "Wesleyan quadrilateral," which identifies Scripture, tradition, reason, and experience as the four sources from which Wesley drew his basic understanding of the Christian faith and life and which we discussed in Chapter 2.

It may be helpful to point out a few of the emphases of "Our Theological Task" in addition to its suggested use of the four sources of Wesleyan theology (Scripture, tradition, reason, and experience).

The document begins with the observation that "Theology is our effort to reflect upon God's gracious action in our lives." It is the purpose of theology to draw us into a deeper relationship with God. Theology helps us to understand "the mysterious reality of God's presence, peace, and power in the world" and to speak and write about our faith more clearly and effectively. Serious theological reflection is both a privilege and an obligation. "Our Theological Task" states:

> As United Methodists, we are called to identify the needs both of individuals and society and to address those needs out of the resources of Christian faith in a way that is clear, convincing, and effective. Theology serves the Church by interpreting the world's needs and challenges to the Church and by interpreting the gospel to the world.

In addition to using the right sources for our theology, we are encouraged to view the theological task as something we do both as individuals and with other Christians, including those of other Christian churches. The theological task is also something essentially practical, informing our decisions and assisting us "to incorporate the promises and demands of the gospel into our daily lives." Wesley referred to this kind of useful theology as "practical divinity." "Our Theological Task" says:

> We endeavor through the power of the Holy Spirit to understand the love of God given in Jesus Christ. We seek to spread this love abroad. As we see more clearly who we have been, as we understand more fully the needs of the world, as we draw more effectively upon our theological heritage, we will become better equipped to fulfill our calling as the people of God.

Works of Piety

The first American Methodist *Discipline* (1785) listed "works of piety" along the very lines that Wesley outlined in several of his writings and in the General Rules for the Methodist societies. It was assumed that discipline was necessary for a growing faith and that God had provided "means of grace" for its nurturing. We will compare a few of the provisions in the first *Discipline* (1785) with what Wesley called "works of piety," which we discussed in Chapter 3.

Methodists were encouraged to "search the scriptures," to read and study the Bible. The 1785 *Discipline* proposed a method for Bible study, suggesting that it be done "constantly," that is, daily. It should also be done "regularly," using a plan of study that will help us to read and appreciate the whole Bible over a period of time, not simply familiarizing ourselves with parts of it. The Bible is to be read "seriously, with Prayer before and after." Readers were advised to read it "carefully," using Wesley's *Explanatory Notes* whenever possible. Most importantly, it must also be read and studied "fruitfully," immediately putting into practice what is learned from the Scriptures.

From their earliest days, Methodists, Evangelicals, and United Brethren generally emphasized the importance of the Bible as the standard for Christian beliefs and conduct. In more recent years they have not always agreed about how the Bible may be considered "the word of God" and the manner in which it is interpreted; but they have valued it, in the words of the present *Book of Discipline*, as "the primary source and criterion" for Christian doctrine and life. United Methodists remain "people of the Book."

Prayer has been a mainstay for the people of the Wesleyan tradition in America. The 1785 *Discipline* urged them to pray privately morning and evening, to pray with their families, and to attend public worship. Prayers were to include thanks to God for their blessings and petitions for their needs. It also admonished them to pray for others.

When Methodists gathered for worship, prayer was a central act of their fellowship. It was critical to the life of the local society or church and to its class meetings. The liturgies included in Wesley's *Sunday Service*, though not widely used in America, were filled with prayers. The long succession of hymnbooks published by the churches for the Wesleyan family were replete with prayers to be sung or said by the congregation.

The 1785 American *Discipline* also emphasized fasting. It asked, "How do you fast every Friday?" and warned that the neglect of fasting would result in "feebleness and faintness" of spiritual life. Omitting fasting "continually grieved" the Holy Spirit. During the nineteenth century, however, the spiritual discipline of fasting came to mean less and less to our forebears. Today we do not usually think of fasting as a spiritual discipline. Its potential as a "means of grace" is worth reconsideration.

Participation in the Lord's Supper was also recommended "at every opportunity" in the 1785 *Discipline*. We have already observed that Wesley received Communion on a frequent basis throughout his adult life. His sermon "The Duty of Constant Communion" spelled out his understanding of the sacrament and his conviction that frequent communing was a principal means of God's conveying grace into the recipient's life. The *Sunday Service of the Methodists in North America* contained an "Order for the Administration of the Lord's Supper."

Celebrations of the Lord's Supper were highly valued among early American Methodists, although they were infrequent—they were generally held four times a year. One of the principal reasons for this was the shortage of ordained clergy to administer the sacrament. Even today, many, perhaps most, congregations celebrate the Lord's Supper only monthly. The preaching service without the Lord's Supper is more customary for public worship than services of preaching with Holy Communion. Wesley might applaud the emphasis on preaching, but he would be baffled by the lack of attention given to the Lord's Supper.

Love feasts and watch night services* were also held regularly in early American Methodism. Joseph Pilmore, one of Wesley's missionary preachers, probably held the first love feast in America in 1770. Following Wesley's pattern, these services included the reading of Scripture, prayer, singing, testimonies, and the sharing of bread and water. Only persons who were serious about their faith were to be admitted to the love feast; at first, only members of the society or earnest prospects were welcome. Love feasts were a means for Christians to share God's love in fellowship, conversation, and with food, without the presence of ordained clergy who are required for celebrations of the Lord's Supper.

Pilmore was also probably the first to conduct a watch night service in America, again in 1770. This was primarily an evening preaching service that lasted several hours, usually until midnight. Besides the sermon, it consisted of Scripture readings, prayers, hymns, and testimonies. Watch night services were sometimes held on New Year's Eve or Day and made use of all or part of Wesley's Covenant Service, a form of which is found in *The United Methodist Book of Worship*. We noted earlier that some congregations still observe love feasts and watch night services, having found them significant means to offer praise to God, undergird faith, deepen Christian fellowship, and equip the participants for mission to the world.

Wesley's people in America also found "Christian conference" an important means of grace. Conversation and fellowship with other Christians was highly prized, and the class meeting was therefore a crucial part of the Methodist structure in America. Everyone was a member of a class, which met weekly under the direction of a class leader. The 1785 *Discipline* was explicit regarding the duties of the leader:

> Let each Leader carefully inquire how every Soul in [the] Class prospers. Not only how each Person observes the outward Rules, but how [the person] grows in the Knowledge and Love of God.

There was concern that the class meetings be "lively and profitable." Class members were to care for one another. While class meetings or similar small groups are an integral part of many churches today, congregations that regularly offer these smaller, intimate associations for spiritual examination, study, and growth are relatively few.

Like their counterparts across the Atlantic, early American Methodists were expected to "avoid evil" in order that they might "go on to perfection." They were warned against wasting time, not keeping the sabbath properly, speaking evil about another member, getting drunk, wearing expensive jewelry and clothing, "laying up treasures upon the earth," incurring debts without intending to repay them, quarreling, and fighting. Everything that did not lead to a more holy life was to be set aside.

From the earliest days Wesley's people in North America were convinced that the Christian life had to be disciplined if it was to be a holy life pleasing to God. "Works of piety" were means of grace given by God to nurture faith and to assist Christians in avoiding evil. "Works of piety" would strengthen the desire and ability to perform "works of mercy."

12-02-02

Works of Mercy

American Methodists were committed to following Wesley by engaging in "works of mercy," doing good to others. This meant caring for the whole person, spiritually, physically, and intellectually. The degree of faithfulness to Wesley's example sometimes varied as we will see. Some areas discussed in the previous chapter show how some Americans followed Wesley's lead.

The most important act of mercy was evangelism: offering the gospel of Christ, the message of God's universal grace, to every person who was willing to listen. To *every* person! There was no discrimination between rich and poor, male and female, educated and uneducated, slave and free—all were created by God, and all were people for whom Christ died. All received God's prevenient (preparing) grace. All stood in need of God's reconciling (justifying) and sustaining (sanctifying) grace. All would discover greater fulfillment and joy—true happiness—by living a holy life conscious of God's presence, undergirding power, and direction. "Our call is to save that which is lost," the Methodists stated; "we cannot expect them to seek *us*. Therefore we should go and seek them." Central to the mission of Wesley's people was the proclamation of the good news of God's grace in Christ through words and deeds.

Methodists organized to extend their ministry of evangelism to every region. They lived in cities, towns, and villages as well as on the frontier. In the earlier days circuit-riding preachers carried the gospel message to even the most remote places. Methodists' concern that people in other nations hear the gospel also prompted them to organize missionary efforts outside the United States. The 1820 General Conference of the Methodist Episcopal Church established the first official missionary organization of the denomination in response to a groundswell of missionary activity. In addition to work in the United States among Native Americans and African Americans, missionary work was begun in Africa (1833), South America (1835), and Asia (1847).

Women were at the forefront of this missionary work, both in the United States and overseas. Between 1869 and 1893, women in all the churches that are now a part of United Methodism formed important home and foreign missionary organizations. Local units of these denominational societies existed in virtually every congregation. These missionary societies were instrumental in educating people about mission work, raising money for the ministry of missionaries, and recruiting people to serve in the field. Wesley never anticipated how far the work he started would spread under the dedicated leadership of women and men who were devoted to the gospel.

American Methodists at first followed their founder in the matter of slavery. Drawing up their first *Discipline*, they clearly stated their intention to eliminate any Methodist participation in the slave trade, saying:

> We . . . therefore think it our most bounden Duty, to take immediately some effectual Method to extirpate this Abomination from among us: And for that purpose we add the following to the Rules of our Society.

One of these rules directed that any Methodist who bought, sold, or gave away slaves was to be expelled immediately from the church, unless such acts were done in order to free these people from their enslavement. Furthermore, a plan was set forth calling for the emancipation of all slaves held by Methodist people, preferably at once, but within no more than five years. Preachers were required to keep a journal recording how their people complied with this plan. Anyone who did not conform was at liberty to withdraw voluntarily from the Methodist fellowship. If someone persisted in failure to comply and did not withdraw, they were to be excluded from membership until they kept the rule.

Unfortunately, Wesley's American followers did not sustain their resolve on the slavery issue. The anti-slavery rule proved especially offensive to southern Methodists, whose economy rested heavily on slave labor. It was left in the hands of individual annual conferences to decide how they would deal with slave holding and trading.

Racism and slavery issues became intense and divisive in the early decades of the nineteenth century. Two of the most tragic instances of racial discrimination occurred in Philadelphia and New York and caused divisions in the Methodist community. In 1787, at Philadelphia's St. George's Methodist Episcopal Church, Richard Allen, a former slave and one of Methodism's heralded African American preachers, became deeply distressed by the congregation's seating practices, which forced African American members to sit apart from whites for worship. Deeply hurt by this and other discriminatory policies, Allen and a number of his African American brothers and sisters walked out of St. George's and in 1816 formed the African Methodist Episcopal Church. In New York's John Street Methodist Episcopal Church, African American members refused to accept the discrimination and segregation imposed on them by the white members. They left John Street and in 1821 formed the African Methodist Episcopal Zion Church.

American Methodists joined vigorously in the debate over abolishing slavery, especially in the 1830's and 1840's. Some Methodists became discouraged and angry that the Methodist Episcopal Church was reluctant to condemn slavery, and they left it to form the Wesleyan Methodist Church in 1843. At the 1844 General Conference of the Methodist Episcopal Church, slavery was bitterly debated. When the argument subsided, the church was seriously divided into northern and southern groups. In 1845, those who favored slavery formed the Methodist Episcopal Church, South. Anti-slavery sentiment also was a key factor in the formation of the Free Methodist Church of North America in 1860.

The Civil War decided the legal question of slavery, but it did not settle the matter of racism in American society and its churches. In the decades following the war, racial discrimination and injustice took such forms as segregated employment practices, housing, public accommodations, and transportation. Restaurants, water fountains, buses and trains, and restrooms had separate facilities for whites and non-whites. Among the ugliest expressions of racism was the lynching of African Americans.

People who most effectively led the fight against racial injustice included women of the Wesleyan tradition. African American woman Ida B. Wells-Barnett condemned lynching as the country's national crime. Thelma Stevens, a white woman from the South, worked tirelessly to bring the church and the nation to recognize and oppose the evil of racism. Methodist and Evangelical United Brethren women were also among those whose views and work resulted in the elimination of the Central Jurisdiction, an institutional form of racial segregation that was built into the Methodist Church in 1939.

The denomination still wrestles with the evil of racism in both the church and the world. United Methodism continues to struggle with what it means to engage in "acts of mercy," to advocate for justice, equality, and peace for all people regardless of their age, gender, handicapping conditions, economic circumstance, and racial or ethnic origins.

American Methodists were intent on encouraging the cultivation of the mind as Wesley taught them. People and preachers were urged to read. If a preacher complained, "But I have no taste for reading," the advice was simply, "Develop a taste for it." They were urged to read "the most useful books" regularly and constantly. At least five hours a day were to be spent in reading and study.

Preachers were also to engage in teaching the faith to their people. They were expected to

> go into every house . . . and teach every one therein, young and old, if they belong to us, to be Christians inwardly and outwardly.
> Make every particular [idea] plain to their understanding; fix it in their memory; write it on their heart. . . .
> Preach expressly on education. [Some may object,] "But I have no gift for this." Gift or no gift, you are to do it; else you are not called to be a Methodist preacher.
> (*A Form of Discipline*, Methodist Episcopal Church, 1791)

Special attention was paid to the instruction of children, "the rising generation." Besides teaching everyone in the home, the preachers were instructed: "Where there are ten children whose parents are in [the] society, meet them an hour once a week; but where this is impracticable, meet them once in two weeks." American Methodists also were enthusiastic supporters of the Sunday school movement. Although the Sunday school included the teaching of adults, it was principally a means for instructing children in the basics of faith and morality. Women have been particularly notable in the origin and development of the Sunday school. It is impossible to imagine its success without the critical role they played in its teaching and leadership.

American Methodists copied Wesley's example by setting up a school, Cokesbury College, named for their first bishops, Thomas Coke and Francis Asbury. The college, located at Abingdon, Maryland, was authorized by the 1784 Christmas Conference. It was meant to educate young people to be productive citizens in their respective communities and faithful Christians in their daily lives. A disastrous fire destroyed Cokesbury in 1795, and rebuilding it proved financially impossible. Since then, however, Methodists, Evangelicals, and United Brethren have continued to recognize the importance of the educational mission of the church, establishing colleges, universities, theological seminaries, and secondary schools in the nineteenth century and later. Presently, more than 100 schools, colleges, universities, and seminaries in the United States are affiliated with The United Methodist Church.

Missions to other lands also included the establishment of schools and colleges. Among them was Isabella Thoburn College in Lucknow, India, named for the first missionary appointed by the Woman's Foreign Missionary Society of the Methodist Episcopal Church. The college has been supported by United Methodist Women's (and predecessor) missionary efforts for over a hundred years. Another is Ewha Woman's University, now the largest women's university in the world.

Just as their founder, John Wesley, made effective use of the publication of books, pamphlets, and magazines, Methodist people in North America also made extensive use of printed materials. The Methodist Book Concern, founded in 1789, was the first denominational publishing house in America. For well over two centuries a wide variety of newspapers, magazines, hymnbooks, disciplines, pamphlets, books, and Sunday school literature have been made available through the denominational presses and bookstores.

Methodists in America also continued to show concern for physical health issues. We noted in Chapter 4 that Wesley taught that the Methodist mission was not only for the spiritual but also for the mental and physical welfare of people. Like their founder, American Wesleyans believed that the body must be cared for as the gift of God. In the early days preachers were urged to see that a copy of Wesley's *Primitive Physick* was made available to every Methodist home. Methodists were advised to be "temperate in all things," that is, not to consume food and drink excessively. They were also warned against drinking too much wine. Far better was to consume water, they were advised.

In the nineteenth century Methodists, Evangelicals, and United Brethren became leaders in the temperance movement, which sought to abolish the production, sale, and consumption of alcoholic beverages. Alcohol was not only detrimental to an individual's health, they believed, but also threatened family welfare and national morality. Women and children suffered the resulting family violence and squandered income. Methodist laywoman Frances E. Willard was among the most active leaders in the American temperance movement.

Following Wesley's example, Methodist leaders and people in America were exhorted to visit the sick, to offer them comfort, and to provide for their necessities whenever there was need.

Commitment to the health and welfare of people effectively bore fruit when hospitals, homes for the elderly, homes for children, and other charitable institutions were opened by Wesleyan churches in the nineteenth century. The first Methodist hospital opened in 1887 in Brooklyn, New York. Missions to other nations often included the provision of medical care and the establishment of hospitals and clinics. Dr. Clara Swain and Isabella Thoburn were sent as missionaries to India in 1869 by the Woman's Foreign Missionary Society of the Methodist Episcopal Church. Dr. Swain is considered the first female physician in India and was an outstanding leader in medical missionary ministry.

Among those who worked hardest among the sick and the poor in the United States and overseas were deaconesses. Methodists, Evangelicals, and United Brethren organized deaconess movements in the late nineteenth century to visit, evangelize, and attend to the needs of the suffering and impoverished. In 1888, the Methodist Episcopal Church officially authorized the office of deaconess in the church. Wesley had seen the potential of women serving in this capacity more than a century earlier and had encouraged them to take up this work as successors to Phoebe, the outstanding leader in the early church mentioned in Romans 16:1. Jane Bancroft Robinson, Lucy Rider Myer, and Belle Harris Bennett were leaders in the Methodist deaconess movement. No group in United Methodist history has been more devoted to carrying out "acts of mercy" than our deaconesses.

Conclusion

John Wesley left his imprint on his people in North America. Wesley's legacy included theological emphases found in the Articles of Religion, sermons, *The Explanatory Notes Upon the New Testament*, and his use of Scripture, tradition, reason, and experience as the guidelines for determining what a Christian should believe and do. His stress on holiness of heart and life, on the inseparability of personal and social religion through the discipline of "works of piety" and "works of mercy," left a lasting mark on his people. Many of these ideas about the Christian faith and life can be found in the 51 hymns written by Charles Wesley, which are included in *The United Methodist Hymnal*.

We have already pointed out that Wesley's people in North America did not always follow his direction. Even in the early years, American Methodists did not feel completely obligated to conform to their founder's views at every point. For example, Asbury would not accept Wesley's appointment as "superintendent" until the American preachers voted to elect him into office. And we have noted that Wesley was disturbed when his "superintendents," Coke and Asbury, were called "bishops" by the American preachers. They set aside Wesley's *Sunday Service* and developed their own informal style of worship. Furthermore, while the American Methodists at first embraced Wesley's abhorrence of slavery, they gradually either tolerated or accepted it as a matter of economic convenience.

The determination of the Americans not to be bound to the wishes and decisions of Wesley regarding their ministry was made clear at the 1787 Conference, when they rescinded their earlier rule binding them to obey him on these matters. While they were still his people in North America, they felt that they understood the unique needs and circumstances of their situation much better than Wesley did and needed to forge their own future.

Some Questions for Reflection and Discussion

1. The early Methodists in America considered evangelism central to their mission. What is evangelism? How is it carried out as part of the mission of our church today?

2. In what ways does your congregation participate in ministries that promote the health and welfare of people in your community, our nation, and the world?

3. American Methodists, Evangelicals, and United Brethren all began overseas mission work in the nineteenth century. What is your understanding of mission work today?

4. American Methodists followed John Wesley's urging that they use prayer as one of the "means of grace" provided by God for spiritual growth. Of what importance is prayer to your life? What resources have you discovered that have benefitted and deepened your experience and use of prayer?

6
CHAPTER

RENEWAL IN THE
WESLEYAN TRADITION

O ne of John Wesley's earliest biographers gives us a description of the Methodist founder's appearance in his later years:

> His face, for an old man, was one of the finest we have seen. A clear, smooth forehead, an aquiline nose [like an eagle's beak], an eye the brightest and most piercing that can be conceived; and a freshness of complexion scarcely ever to be found at his years, and impressive of the most perfect health conspired to render him a venerable and interesting figure. Few have seen him without being struck with his appearance; and many who had been greatly prejudiced against him have been known to change their opinion the moment they have been introduced into his presence. . . . In dress, he was a pattern of neatness and simplicity. A narrow, plaited stock [a neckcloth worn by clergy]; a coat with a small upright collar; no buckles at his knees; no silk or velvet in any part of his apparel, and a head as white as snow, gave an idea of something primitive and apostolic; while an air of neatness and cleanliness was diffused over his whole person.
>
> (John Hampson, *Memoirs of the Late Rev. John Wesley*, 1791)

From other contemporary descriptions we may conclude that Wesley was a small man. His slight build, however, is no indication of the extensive influence he exerted in his time, even with his many faults and peculiarities. Some have claimed that he and his Methodist people in England were responsible for such sweeping social change that they prevented the sort of bloody revolution that engulfed France in the final years of the eighteenth century. Others believe this assessment is exaggerated and have criticized Wesley for not doing enough to advance sound religion and effective social reform. There is little doubt, however, that Wesley's life and ministry left a major impression on England, not only during his lifetime but long after his death. His life and theology moved many English Methodists to become leaders in changing the spiritual and social climate of their nation for decades following his demise. His influence is also apparent in North America and other parts of the world where people followed his understanding of the Christian faith and his commitment to organize people for spiritual growth and ministry.

What can we learn from Wesley that can help us to be the faithful people God intends? Some have said that we need to "go back to Wesley." It may be more correct to say that in many ways we need "to catch up with Wesley." In his devotion to the prisoner, the poor, and the suffering he is out in front of us, bidding us to be more caring and compassionate in both our words and actions. We also have great difficulty matching the balance of evangelism and social action, reason and experience in religion, and preaching and the sacraments that he achieved.

Some of Wesley's ideas and practices, of course, would not be appropriate for our time. Most of the cures in *Primitive Physick* are antiquated. His views on raising and educating children are harsh and outdated. Some of his judgments about Roman Catholicism are no longer accurate or appropriate. Yet in spite of these limitations, there is still much he can teach us.

Perhaps Wesley's deepest concern about us today would be our *casual Christianity*. Our commitment to Christ is often based on what is convenient for us. We do not want our faith to be too demanding or embarrassing. We want it to benefit us and to make us feel good, without the self-denial and change that it often requires. If there is anything that impresses us about John Wesley, it is his dedication, by the grace of God, to be an "altogether Christian" as opposed to an "almost Christian" (see his sermon titled "The Almost Christian," 1741). Like Wesley, we need to be renewed together by the presence of the God of grace and power. We know that God is always seeking to renew us in our thinking together (theology), our living together (works of piety), and our serving together (works of mercy).

Thinking Together in the Presence of the God of Grace: Theology

How we think about our faith is important; it is the basis for understanding, expressing, and acting on the gospel. It is the groundwork for our living and serving Christ together. If we are to address the complex, challenging issues and decisions that confront us personally and socially, we need to know what we believe and how to relate life's issues to those beliefs.

John Wesley gave his people a set of doctrinal standards that contain what he considered to be the main beliefs of Christianity and, therefore, of Methodism. We have described them in previous chapters. They are the Articles of Religion that he sent to America in 1784, his sermons, and *The Explanatory Notes Upon the New Testament*. We have also noted that Wesley derived these three theological standards from the four principal sources of Scripture, tradition, reason, and experience.

The Articles, sermons, and *Explanatory Notes* show that Wesley held that some doctrines form the core of Christianity. He considered them essential beliefs on which he thought there was general agreement in the church. They were clearly set out in Scripture, clarified in the tradition of the church, tested by reason, and confirmed by experience. Among these essentials are a Trinitarian* understanding of God; acknowledgment of the widespread nature and seriousness of sin; dependence on the preparing (prevenient), accepting (justifying), and sustaining (sanctifying and perfecting) grace of God; Jesus' death as the means by which we are reconciled to God; and the work of the Holy Spirit, who cultivates in us holiness of heart and life. Christians, Wesley believed, should be agreed on these central affirmations of their faith.

In his sermon titled "Catholic Spirit" (1750) and in other places, Wesley also spoke about what he called "opinions." These are theological views that he considered of less importance than the essentials. On matters of "opinion" there are differences among believers. For example, how baptism is administered and how churches are organized are not theologically central to Christianity. "As to all opinions which do not strike at the root of Christianity, we [Methodists] 'think and let think,' " he wrote (*The Character of a Methodist*, 1742).

> All men will not see all things alike. It is an unavoidable consequence of the present weakness and shortness of human understanding that several men will be of several minds, in religion as well as common life. So it has been from the beginning of the world, and so it will be 'till the restitution of all things.
>
> (Sermon, "Catholic Spirit," 1750)

Wesley may have hoped that people would come to "see all things alike" in religion and theology, but he certainly felt that people must be free to decide for themselves what they believe. Under no circumstances should they be forced. He wrote that:

> everyone must follow the dictates of his own conscience in simplicity and godly sincerity. He must be fully persuaded in his own mind, and then act accordingly to the best light he has.
>
> (Sermon, "Catholic Spirit," 1750)

Wesley urged that Christians act in a "catholic" or universal spirit toward one another. In spite of doctrinal and other serious differences, they must love each other, acting with patience and kindness, without "jealousy and evil surmising." They should commend to God in prayer all with whom they differ and kindle in others "love and good works." Wesley urged that we love those with whom we differ "in deed and in truth."

In saying that people should act in love toward one another in spite of their theological differences, Wesley did not support the view that "anything goes" theologically. While people of a "catholic spirit" are not rigidly dogmatic on every matter of Christian doctrine, especially "opinions," neither are they indifferent about the central affirmations of Christian faith. Wesley commented:

> A man of a truly catholic spirit has not now his religion to seek. He is fixed as the sun in his judgment concerning the main branches of Christian doctrine.... Go first and learn the first elements of the gospel of Christ, and then you shall learn to be of a truly catholic spirit.
>
> (Sermon, "Catholic Spirit," 1750)

John Wesley was not indifferent to theological views that he considered misleading and dangerous. We have mentioned previously that he entered into serious and heated theological debates with predestinarians, who denied that human beings have free will, and with Deists, who felt that God was uninterested and uninvolved in people's daily life. Wesley never hesitated to challenge theological views that did not serve to bring people into a deeper relationship with God and fit them for effective ministry in the world. But when he disputed with others or defended himself in theological matters, he usually did all he could to avoid malicious acts and spiteful language. Wherever possible he invited those who held other theological views to enter into dialogue with him and with one another and to seek mutual resolution of their disagreement.

We can summarize Wesley's views on theological diversity as follows: In essential beliefs, let there be unity. In those things that are not essential, let there be freedom. In all things, let there be love.

The Book of Discipline of The United Methodist Church, Part II, "Doctrinal Standards and Our Theological Task," shows that our church is not only rooted in doctrinal ideas and standards that have come to us from Wesley and our denominational experience in North America but is also committed to theological exploration. The section "Our Theological Task," which we have mentioned previously, acknowledges that the mystery of God's presence and activity and the emerging issues of our personal and social life require us to engage in serious theological thought using Scripture, tradition, reason, and experience.

"Our Theological Task" encourages us to think about our faith as we are anchored in the historic doctrines and standards of our church, such as the Articles of Religion, Wesley's sermons and *Explanatory Notes*, and The Confession of Faith of the Evangelical United Brethren Church. These are historic boundaries within which we express together our faith and its implications for our daily living. But "Our Theological Task" also includes testing our doctrinal views and statements, our boundaries, in the light of new insights based on the Bible, tradition, reason, and experience. For that reason the document states:

> While the [United Methodist] Church considers its doctrinal affirmations a central feature of its identity and restricts official changes to a constitutional process, the Church encourages serious reflection across the theological spectrum. (*The Book of Discipline, 1996*, page 72)

It seems, therefore, that we are encouraged to understand the relationship between our "doctrinal standards" and "Our Theological Task" as one of creative tension. The standards set the boundaries within which our theological task is to be carried out. But engaging in this theological task may raise questions about the adequacy of some points in these boundaries and even challenge them. Taken seriously, this issue may create considerable theological controversy among us.

In conclusion, we must point out again that John Wesley did not consider theology simply a matter of theory or speculation. He called it "practical divinity" because it is the foundation for our words and acts, the basis for holiness of heart and life.

Living Together in the Presence of the God of Grace: Works of Piety

In 1742, Wesley published a short pamphlet titled "The Character of a Methodist," in which he described several characteristics of the typical Methodist. He began by saying:

> a Methodist is one who has "the love of God shed abroad in his heart by the Holy Ghost given unto him" [*Romans 5:5*]; one who "loves the Lord his God with all his heart, and with all his soul, and with all his mind, and with all his strength" [*Mark 12:30*]. God is the joy of his heart, and the desire of his soul, which is constantly crying out, "Whom have I in heaven but thee? and there is none upon earth that I desire beside thee! My God and my all! Thou art the strength of my heart, and my portion for ever!" [*Psalm 73:25-26*]

He proceeded to list a number of marks of the Methodist life.

1. Methodists are "happy in God." They rejoice because they have found forgiveness in Christ (*Ephesians 1:7*). The Holy Spirit is present in their lives assuring them that they are children of God (*Romans 8:16*).

2. In everything Methodists give thanks, knowing that they can trust God even in the most distressing and trying situations (*1 Peter 5:7*). They know that God cares for them and will deliver them.

3. Methodists pray without ceasing (*1 Thessalonians 5:17*). Even when they are not in a church or on their knees in private prayer, they continually walk with God (*1 John 1:7*); and their hearts are "ever lifted up to God, at all times, and in all places."

4. As they love God, Methodists also love their neighbors (*1 John 4:21*). Their hearts are full of love for everyone. They love their enemies, even "the evil and the unthankful" enemies of God (*Luke

6:35). This love is constant. It continues even when it is rejected by those who are loved.

5. Methodists are "pure in heart" (*Matthew 5:8*). The love of God has purified their hearts "from all revengeful passions, from envy, malice, and wrath, from every unkind" attitude and feeling.

6. A Methodist has one focus: doing God's will (*John 6:38*).

7. Methodists avoid evil (one of the General Rules of the Methodist Societies). They especially refrain from words and acts that might hurt others.

8. They do good to all—neighbors, strangers, friends, and enemies (another of the General Rules).

How can Methodists live this type of life? Wesley had two answers to this question. First, it is impossible to live it apart from the grace of God, which renews and constantly resupplies our lives. God makes his grace available in a number of ways. We noted some of them in Chapter 3 when we discussed "works of piety" and the "means of grace." They include Bible study, prayer, fasting, Christian conversation, the Lord's Supper, and private and public worship. These are God's gifts that energize us for holy living. We cannot be the kind of people God intends without constantly opening our lives to the God of grace and using the means of grace God offers us in a disciplined fashion.

Second, we need the company of others to live the holy life. Wesley was persuaded that it is extremely difficult, if not impossible, to live faithfully without the encouragement and companionship of other Christians. The early network of Methodist societies, bands, and classes under Wesley's supervision formed a "connection" of believers with God, with Wesley, and with one another. This "connection" gave identity to the Methodist movement, provided a community for spiritual growth, and promoted mission more effectively. Methodists could do together what would have been practically unattainable individually.

United Methodists today realize the importance of being connected to God and one another, a concept that has deep biblical roots (see

John 15:1-11; Romans 12:1-8). Our United Methodist connection includes every individual affiliated with our church, every local congregation, our districts, annual conferences, Jurisdictions and Central Conferences, the general agencies of the church, and other denominational organizations, and the General Conference. More broadly, it also includes our brothers and sisters in other churches that come from Wesleyan roots and other denominations that share with us a common loyalty to Jesus Christ.

Like Wesley, The United Methodist Church also understands that our living together in the presence of the God of grace means that we must be an inclusive fellowship. Our commitment to this principle is stated in the church's Constitution.

> All persons, without regard to race, color, national origin, status, or economic condition, shall be eligible to attend its worship services, to participate in its programs, and, when they take the appropriate vows, to be admitted into its membership in any local church in the connection. In The United Methodist Church no conference or other organizational unit of the Church shall be structured so as to exclude any member or any constituent body of the Church because of race, color, national origin, status, or economic condition.
>
> (*The Book of Discipline, 1996*, page 22)

There are a number of matters about which we should be concerned regarding our life together. One of them is that we are not always faithful to the principle of inclusiveness that we say governs our church life. Our local churches and other levels of our connection do not always invite the participation of everyone who wishes to join us. When it comes to inclusiveness, we do not always practice what we say we believe.

Another concern is that too many of our congregations do not provide the encouragement, care, and support that people need to weather the storms and crises of faith that we all experience at one time or another. How do we help people cope with their burdens of guilt, sorrow, anger, failure, and fear? The Methodist classes offered personal support and loving care to their members. How can we embody that quality of Christian fellowship in our time? Finally, how can we better serve those in need?

Charles Wesley wrote a hymn that expresses our prayer that the God of grace assist us in holy living together in Christ:

Christ, from whom all blessings flow,
    perfecting the saints below,
hear us, who thy nature share,
    who thy mystic body are.

Join us, in one spirit join,
    let us still receive of thine;
still for more on thee we call,
    thou who fillest all in all.

Move and actuate and guide,
    diverse gifts to each divide;
placed according to thy will,
    let us all our work fulfill.

Many are we now, and one,
    we who Jesus have put on;
there is neither bond nor free,
    male nor female, Lord, in thee.

Love, like death, hath all destroyed,
    rendered all distinctions void;
names and sects and parties fall;
    thou, O Christ, art all in all.
("Christ, From Whom All Blessings Flow,"
The United Methodist Hymnal, 550)

Serving Together in the Presence of the God of Grace: Works of Mercy

On June 25, 1744, John Wesley held the first conference of his British Methodist preachers. Six persons were present at the Foundry Chapel in London, including John and Charles Wesley. The minutes of the meeting show that after praying together, the preachers considered three subjects: "1. What to teach; 2. How to teach, and 3. What to do. . . ." The last topic dealt with how the Methodists under Wesley's leadership planned to integrate their doctrine, discipline, and practice of the Christian faith. Their consideration of theology and organization was not complete until they actively responded to what God called them to do.

The vision of the early British Methodists regarding their mission was far-ranging. In one place it was stated in question and answer form. Question: "What may we reasonably believe to be God's design in raising up the Preachers [and people] called Methodists?" Answer: "Not to form any new sect; but to reform the nation, particularly the Church; and to spread scriptural holiness over the land." When the Methodists in North America organized the Methodist Episcopal Church in 1784, they stated the mission of their new church in similar terms. Its purpose was "To Reform the Continent and to spread scriptural holiness over these lands." This was an ambitious goal. How could it be accomplished? Wesley's answer was simple: supported by God's love available through the means of grace, we participate in reform and spread scriptural holiness by avoiding evil and doing good. These are two sides of the same coin. Avoiding evil means putting aside words and acts that hurt our neighbors, endanger our health and spiritual welfare, and offend God. Doing good states the matter more positively. It takes form as we serve God together by engaging in "acts of mercy."

In the important pamphlet "The Character of a Methodist" (1742), Wesley completed his list of the marks of the Methodist life by saying that a Methodist

> does good unto all . . . [Galatians 6:10]—unto neighbors, and strangers, friends, and enemies. And that in every possible kind; not only to their bodies, by "feeding the hungry, clothing the naked, visiting those that are sick or in prison" [Matthew 25:35-36], but much more [do they] labour to do good to their souls, as of the ability which God giveth [1 Peter 4:11]: to awaken those that sleep in death; to bring those that are awakened to the atoning blood, that "being satisfied by faith" [Romans 5:1] they may have peace with God; and to provoke those who have peace with God to abound more in love and in good works.

Wesley was convinced that genuine Christian ministry, doing good to all in the name of Christ, gave attention to the whole person, body and soul. He exhorted his people to do the same.

We have already noted how Wesley spent his own life and resources for the welfare of others, especially the poor. He was concerned about where and how they lived and whether they possessed at least the basic necessities and opportunities of life. Where he detected need, he not only proposed a plan to meet it but also spent his energy and money to carry it out.

At their best, Wesley's people have followed his example in doing good to others in the name of Christ by caring about their physical and spiritual health and welfare. The Social Principles of The United Methodist Church testify to our concern about the whole person and the whole human race. The Preamble to the Social Principles reads in part:

> We acknowledge our complete dependence upon God in birth, in life, in death, and in life eternal. Secure in God's love, we affirm the goodness of life and confess our many sins against God's will for us as we find it in Jesus Christ. We have not always been faithful stewards of all that has been committed to us by God the Creator. We have been reluctant followers of Jesus Christ in his mission to bring all persons into a community of love. Though called by the Holy Spirit to become new creatures in Christ, we have resisted the further call to become the people of God in our dealings with each other and the earth on which we live.
>
> (*The Book of Discipline, 1996*, page 85)

United Methodists participate in a wide variety of ministries that show that we do more than merely talk about mission to others. We have soup kitchens and food pantries to feed the hungry. We participate in community shelters for abused women and children. Our prison chaplains and visitors provide a caring presence to the imprisoned. We establish hospitals and homes for the elderly. Some of us are visitors and counselors, offering the love of Christ through our words and acts, in health and welfare facilities and agencies in our communities. Many of our congregations offer programs to strengthen marriages and to show support to divorced people, widows and widowers, and one-parent families. Others are active in ministries to people with AIDS. We have community centers that provide recreation, daycare, youth employment programs, English as a second language for immigrants, and advocacy for persons with disabilities. We continue to support schools, colleges, and universities.

Through mission work in the United States and other countries, we have learned that advocacy is important in attacking the root causes of poverty and social ills. Wesley identified apathy and exploitation by the wealthy and the widespread sale and consumption of alcoholic beverages as some of the principal sources of spiritual and social sin. United Methodists have continued that tradition by resisting injustice against women, minorities, children, and the poor. Seemingly secular campaigns like divestment in South Africa and product boycotts have addressed deep social sins.

We evangelize in our pulpits, homes, communities, work places, and wherever we are by words and acts that announce God's judgment on sin, forgiveness in Christ, and new life in the Holy Spirit. We are not the body of Christ unless we clearly and boldly announce where we miss the mark of doing what is just and right and declare the good news of reconciliation and abundant living in Christ (*John 10:10*).

Many of us are not aware of the countless ways we share in doing good to others. In addition to the ministries of our local churches, we also participate in ministries beyond our neighborhoods and communities. Where we cannot be present ourselves to offer care, we support others who are doing good on our behalf in the name of Christ. Our gifts extend our serving together to other communities in our nation and world. We minister through others to the physical and spiritual needs of people by proclaiming the gospel, supporting ministries of health and healing, and serving as advocates for justice and social change.

We can do more good to others in both our words and acts. We can be more sensitive to our neighbors' circumstances and needs. We can speak the words and do the deeds that announce God's judgment on unrighteousness and bring hope and healing. We can practice more thoroughly Wesley's advice on the use of money. We probably "make all we can"; perhaps we "save all we can"; but it is unlikely that we "give all we can."

We serve together in the presence of the God of grace. Charles Wesley's words give us direction and express our fervent prayer:

> Forth in thy name, O Lord, I go,
>   my daily labor to pursue;
> thee, only thee, resolved to know
>   in all I think or speak or do.
>
> The task thy wisdom hath assigned,
>   O let me cheerfully fulfill;
> in all my works thy presence find,
>   and prove thy good and perfect will.
>
> Thee may I set at my right hand,
>   whose eyes mine inmost substance see,

and labor on at thy command,
and offer all my works to thee.

For thee delightfully employ
whate'er thy bounteous grace hath given;
and run my course with even joy,
and closely walk with thee to heaven.
("Forth in Thy Name, O Lord,"
The United Methodist Hymnal, 438)

Conclusion

John Wesley gives us a pattern for theological, spiritual, and missional renewal in both his words and acts. He reminds us that God seeks to bring us to holiness of heart and life, which is the true substance of Christian faith. Holiness of heart and life is personal; but it is not achieved apart from the preparing, accepting, and sustaining grace of God. It is not realized apart from the fellowship and partnership of our sisters and brothers in the faith. And it is never complete until we love God and our neighbors with the same kind of love with which God loves us.

Some Questions for Reflection and Discussion

1. How can we learn from John Wesley's model for discussion with those with whom we have theological differences?

2. What do you consider to be the "essential" theological ideas of the Christian faith?

3. What does it mean to be what Wesley called an "altogether Christian" as opposed to what he called an "almost Christian"?

4. How has this book challenged you to be a different person? If it has encouraged you to make changes in your life, how do you intend to make them?

GLOSSARY

ANGLICAN CHURCH The Church of England, formed in the sixteenth century Reformation under King Henry VIII and Queen Elizabeth I. It rejected papal authority, allowed clergy to marry, and used the English language for Scriptures and services in its prayer book and its Authorized (known as King James) Version of the Bible. The Anglican church recognizes three orders of clergy: bishops, priests, and deacons and permits ordinations only by bishops. John and Charles Wesley and their father Samuel were all ordained priests in the Anglican church.

ANTINOMIAN Literally means, "against the law." This understanding of the Christian life emphasized salvation by faith alone and minimized the place of rules, disciplines, and good works.

ARMINIAN Name given to Christians who followed the teaching of Jacob Arminius (1560–1609), a Dutch theologian who affirmed the freedom of all people by God's grace to repent and receive God's forgiveness. John Wesley considered his theology to follow Arminian principles.

ARTICLES OF RELIGION A set of theological statements John Wesley sent to North America with his *Sunday Service* in 1784. They are recognized as "doctrinal standards" and are printed in *The Book of Discipline of The United Methodist Church*. Wesley simplified the Thirty-Nine Articles of the Church of England into twenty-four, and American Methodists added a twenty-fifth.

ASSURANCE A main theme of Wesley's theology that holds that we can be confident that we are children of God through the presence and witness of the Holy Spirit in our lives.

BANDS Small groups of Methodists similar to classes but composed of members who were considered more spiritually mature.

BOOK OF COMMON PRAYER The official prayerbook of the Church of England, drafted in the sixteenth century. John Wesley used it for worship and as a pattern for the *Sunday Service* he sent to North America. It contains services and Scripture readings for daily Morning and Evening Prayer and Holy Communion, along with occasional services such as marriage and burial. Its Scripture readings were taken from a 1536 translation of the Bible, not the King James Version.

CHRISTIAN CONFERENCE A means of grace associated with works of piety that meant sharing with others in Christian conversation and fellowship.

CLASSES Small groups of Methodists who met weekly for prayer, fellowship, and Bible study. The numbers of members varied.

CONNECTION Usually refers to the entire organization of The United Methodist Church. The term originally was used to describe the preachers and people "in connection" with John Wesley.

COVENANT SERVICE An order of worship based on Puritan church practice, adapted by Wesley for use by the Methodist people to remind them of God's covenant with them and their covenant with God. A "Service of Covenant Renewal" is found in *The United Methodist Book of Worship*.

DEISM A theological movement that attempted to construct a reasonable religion. It held that God is aloof from the world and questioned some of the traditional beliefs of Christianity such as the miracle stories in the Bible.

DOCTRINAL STANDARDS Statements of the basic theological views of The United Methodist Church that include the Articles of Religion, Wesley's sermons and *Explanatory Notes Upon the New Testament*, and the Confession of Faith of the Evangelical United Brethren Church.

ENTHUSIASM Used in Wesley's day as a term of abuse for emotional religious extremism or fanaticism.

GERMAN PIETISM A movement in the seventeenth and eighteenth centuries that emphasized personal religious experience based on prayer, contemplation, and Bible study.

HOLINESS OF HEART AND LIFE A life filled with the grace of God that is devoted to complete love for God and neighbor. According to John Wesley, it is the goal of every Christian.

JUSTIFICATION BY FAITH God's pardoning and accepting love made available through belief in the life, death, and resurrection of Jesus.

LOVE FEAST A service that was adapted by Wesley from the Moravians at which there is singing, praying, testifying to God's grace, and sharing bread and water (or other food) as a sign of Christian love for one another.

METHODIST Name given to one of the groups centrally involved in the eighteenth century English evangelical revival. The name eventually came to be more specifically related to the group of people who looked to John and Charles Wesley as their leaders.

NEW BIRTH The work of grace that God does in us, resulting in new life lived under the presence and power of the Holy Spirit.

"OUR THEOLOGICAL TASK" Document in Part II of *The Book of Discipline of The United Methodist Church* that encourages thought and reflection on our faith using Scripture, tradition, reason, and experience.

PIETISTS See German Pietism.

PREDESTINATION A doctrine based on Romans 8:29 that many in Wesley's day and since believe. It teaches that people are not free to accept or reject God's offer of salvation; God has already decreed who is to be forgiven and who is not. Wesley rejected this idea, holding that by the prevenient grace of God everyone is free to decide on this matter.

PREVENIENT GRACE Literally means the grace that "comes before." It is the grace of God that is "free in all and free for all" and makes possible for everyone further response to God's forgiving and reconciling grace.

108

QUADRILATERAL Literally, a four-sided figure. The Wesleyan quadrilateral is the four sources we rely on for what we should believe and do. They include Scripture, tradition, reason, and experience. Of these, Scripture is considered primary.

SIN The deepest problem in human nature. The Greek word in the New Testament means, literally, "missing the mark." Most fundamentally sin is setting up our own will as paramount, instead of seeking God's will. Sin therefore includes doing what God forbids and not doing what God requires. Christ's sacrifice atones for the sins of humanity and makes forgiveness possible.

SOCIETIES The earliest basic unit of Methodism organized by Wesley for worship, preaching, and fellowship.

TRINITARIAN One who accepts the central doctrine of the Christian faith, that the one God exists in three persons (the Trinity). Traditionally, and during Wesley's time, these are the Father, the Son, and the Holy Spirit (Ghost). Jesus Christ is the incarnation of God the Son, the second person of the Trinity.

WATCH NIGHT An evening worship service that includes prayer and singing. It came to be held on New Year's Eve or Day. The liturgy of the Covenant Renewal Service has often been used for this gathering.

STUDY
GUIDE

Ruth A. Daugherty

INTRODUCTION

This study guide provides suggestions and resources for study leaders of *John Wesley: Holiness of Heart and Life.* The focus of the guide is (1) to consider the interrelatedness of Wesley's spirituality and theology and his practice of Christian faith, (2) to relate these understandings to our personal lives, and (3) to explore the implications for our church in mission.

The Book of Discipline of The United Methodist Church, 1996 (page 46) makes reference to the centrality of Wesley's teaching about the interrelatedness of faith and works:

> No motif in the Wesleyan tradition has been more constant than the link between Christian doctrine and Christian living. Methodists have always been strictly enjoined to maintain the unity of faith and good works through the means of grace. . . . The coherence of faith with ministries of love forms the discipline of Wesleyan spirituality and Christian discipleship.

This guide includes plans for six sessions. Each session relates to one of the six chapters in the book; the chapter sequence follows the text. Each session has a statement of purpose and several objectives. Suggestions for preparing the classroom, worship, discussion in small groups ("classes"), learning activities, and participant assignments may be adapted for various needs and situations.

PREPARING TO BE A STUDY LEADER

A study leader provides opportunities for group members to learn through the use of various resources and activities. Information you glean from reading and your personal experiences can be shared with the group. Do this in brief time segments, with opportunity for response or sharing from the members of the group. In this study particularly, participants need to have learning experiences involving both head and heart.

Steps for Preparing to Be a Study Leader:

1. Seek God's help and presence in prayer.

2. Get an overview of the book. Read the introduction to the book and become familiar with the table of contents.

3. Read the book for the general flow.

4. Scan the suggested purposes and objectives for each session in the Study Guide.

5. Become familiar with the basic resources in addition to the book (the Bible; *The United Methodist Book of Worship; The United Methodist Hymnal; The Book of Discipline, 1996; The Book of Resolutions*).

6. Review the bibliography. Buy or borrow as many of the books as you are able to read. Some may be available at your public library or through interlibrary lending. Clergy or others interested in Wesley may have some of the resources. Reading as widely as possible will help you be better prepared to lead and will give you a feeling of confidence.

7. Reread the book and the study guide. Make notes about items to include in plans for your group. Add your own ideas.

8. Make an outline for each session. Develop details with allotments of time, especially for the first session or two. Make adjustments after each session to allow for flexibility to pursue issues or activities that may become important.

9. Note the special items or display materials you will need to prepare ahead of time for a particular session.

PLANNING THE SESSIONS

Common Elements in Each Session

1. *Hymns.* Music and singing have been present in Methodism since its beginning. Hymns were used for Christian instruction. *The United Methodist Hymnal* has fifty-one hymns written by Charles Wesley, one by Samuel Wesley, and several translated by John Wesley (see Index of Composers, and so forth, page 922). Some of these hymns are suggested for study session worship.

2. *Scripture.* Study of the Bible was one of the disciplines that Wesley practiced. Scripture readings suggested for worship include commentary from Wesley's *Explanatory Notes Upon the New Testament.*

3. *Prayers* used in each session are from *John Wesley's Prayers,* edited by Frederick C. Gill, London: The Epworth Press, 1951, reprinted in 1959. Gill indicates that these prayers are taken from Wesley's first prayer book—his earliest publication (1733)—and from his later works, including revised editions of Wesley's other manuals of devotion.

4. *Class Meetings.* Persons involved in the Methodist movement were members of "classes" that met regularly. It is suggested that small groups ("classes") be formed during the first session and be used for discussions and activities in each session. Use the question/topic suggested in the Study Guide or the ones at the end of each chapter in the text.

5. *Quotes.* Some quotes from John Wesley pertaining to the theme of each chapter are included in the session plans.

6. *Timeline of John Wesley's Life and Era.* In the first session, a Timeline is begun that is added to in later sessions. The Timeline should be displayed throughout the sessions to show the relationship of time and events in Wesley's life.

Classroom Setting: Meet in a room other than an auditorium or sanctuary, if possible.

1. *Arrangement of chairs.* Create an atmosphere of openness and community. Chairs arranged in a circle, concentric circles, or semicircle(s) encourage active participation. Allow open space for movement and activities.

2. *Displays.* Pictures, quotes, or posters related to the study will help to provide a setting that is inviting and set the tone for the sessions. Place them on the walls with masking tape (if this is permissible), bulletin boards, or on large sheets of paper placed on a wall. Provide space visible to all group members for the Timeline.

3. *Supplies.* Chalkboard and chalk or an easel with newsprint pad and markers. *The United Methodist Hymnal* for every group member. (Ask class members to bring one or make arrangements to borrow them.) Have sufficient copies of materials you may plan to use in the sessions. (For example, "tickets" for the class members in Session III). Quotes should be written large enough to be read. Prepare the Timeline in advance on shelf paper or sheets of newsprint.

4. *Personal comfort.* Inform group members of location of restrooms and provide comfort breaks. Check room temperature.

5. *Checklist.* Make a checklist for yourself for each session.

PARTICIPATING GROUP MEMBERS

Learning Process

Access: Obtain information through reading and activities.

Assimilate: Bring together new information and understandings with past experiences and learnings.

Act: Use what has been learned in some tangible, intentional, and meaningful way.

People learn more readily for themselves, gathering information that can be related to what they already know. Use different methods for presenting material. Involve participants in a variety of activities to reinforce what has been learned. Provide opportunities for group members to share from their wealth of experiences and knowledge. Urge them to take some kind of action using what they have learned.

Assignment

Basic: Book and Bible readings for each session

Enrichment Opportunities: Recommended readings or activities provided to enhance the learning process for group members

● Personal disciplines:

—Read the Bible each day
—Keep a journal
—Fast one day/one meal a week
—Reflect on presence of God frequently during the day

● Pray prayers of John Wesley morning and evening:

Morning: "Thou has mercifully kept us the last night; blessed be thy continued goodness. Receive us likewise into Thy protection this day. Guide and assist us in all our thoughts, words, and actions. Amen."

Evening: "And now, as we lay ourselves down to sleep, take us into Thy gracious protection and settle our spirits in quiet thoughts of Thy glory. Amen."

● Love Feast Service for group (Session 3)

● Sarah Crosby "visits" the group to tell her story. (Session 3)

- Implications of Social Principles of The United Methodist Church for guidance for Christians in doing "Works of Mercy" (Session 4)

- Interviewer and three women to be interviewed (Session 4)

- "Parade of Saints" (Session 5)

- Deaconess movement in Methodism and some prominent leaders (Session 5)

- Covenant Renewal Service (Session 6)

PROVIDING OPTIONS FOR STUDY

The study is designed for six sessions to last approximately two hours each. Select and/or modify proposals for the needs of your group. If less than six sessions are held, make plans to cover as many of the themes as possible.

Sessions may be held over a period of weeks, a one-day study, in adult Sunday school classes or coffee klatsches. Whatever time is used, urge each participant to read this book, *John Wesley: Holiness of Heart and Life*.

STUDY SESSION 1

Purpose: To provide information and opportunities to learn about the life and times of John Wesley.

Objectives
- To build community through activities related to the study;
- To establish the framework for the study;
- To review resources;
- To involve group members in learning activities about the life and times of John Wesley.

Preparing for the Session

- Materials needed for activities: Information for one or more of the activities used under Community Building; information about events and persons for the Timeline; "tickets" for class meetings; copies of the Morning and Evening Prayers by John Wesley for each one who wishes to use them as an Enrichment Opportunity (see the Introduction, page 116)

- Make a poster with quotes from John Wesley for guidance. Place on a bulletin board or wall to hang throughout all class sessions:

  —"The wisest men [people] 'know' but 'in part.' " (Sermon, "The Imperfection of Human Knowledge")
  —"Treat me as you would desire to be treated yourself upon a change of circumstance."
  —"No one, then, is so perfect in this life, as to be free from ignorance." (Sermon, "Christian Perfection")
  —"For how far is love, even with many wrong opinions, to be preferred before truth itself without love!" (Preface to Sermons)

● Post the list of **Enrichment Opportunities** listed in the Introduction (pages 116-17) with sessions in which each is to be shared with the group. Allow space for persons to sign their names by each specific activity.

Opening Worship

Hymn: "O For a Thousand Tongues to Sing" (*The United Methodist Hymnal*, 57)

Scripture: Luke 4:18-19 (Reader 1, Scripture; Reader 2, *Explanatory Notes Upon the New Testament,* by John Wesley)

Reader 1: "He hath anointed me . . . "

Reader 2: ". . . with the Spirit. He hath, by the power of His Spirit which dwelleth in Me, set Me apart for these offices."

Reader 1: "To preach the gospel to the poor . . . "

Reader 2: ". . . literally and spiritually. How is the doctrine of the ever-blessed Trinity interwoven even in those Scriptures where one would least expect it! How clear a declaration of the great Three-One is there in those very words: 'The *Spirit* of the *Lord* is upon *me*'!"

Reader 1: "To proclaim deliverance to the captives, and recovery of sight to the blind, to set at liberty them that are bruised."

Prayer: "Help us to see Thy power, to own Thy presence, to admire Thy wisdom, and to love Thy goodness in all Thy creatures; and by all, draw our hearts still nearer to Thee. Such mercy and grace we beg for ourselves, and all ours and Thine everywhere, is our great Mediator's blessed word: *Our Father,* etc." (John Wesley)

Community Building Activities

Activity 1: "A Significant Event in My Faith Journey"

Give each person a copy of "A Significant Event in My Faith Journey" (which follows) and allow five minutes for written responses. Ask persons to find a partner, introduce themselves, and share some of their responses. Then ask everyone to introduce her/his partner and to share one aspect of the person's faith journey.

A Significant Event in My Faith Journey

1. A significant event in my faith journey was . . .
2. What was the setting in which this event occurred?
3. Picture the person(s), if any, who were involved.
4. Reflect upon the change this made in your life.

Activity 2: "Who Am I?"

Give each person a slip of paper with the name of or information about a person who was part of the life of John Wesley. Have each person find the match to the name or information. After matches are made, ask persons to introduce themselves to their partner. Then have partners introduce each other to the group and share information from slips of paper.

> Samuel Wesley—Rector at Epworth and father of John Wesley
> Susanna Annesley Wesley—mother of John Wesley
> Charles Wesley—younger brother of John; closest friend and ally
> Emilia, Susanna, Mary, Mehatabel, Anne, Martha, Kezia—seven sisters of John Wesley who survived to maturity
> Sophia Hopkey—a parishioner in Georgia with whom John had a disastrous romance
> Grace Murray—Methodist widow whom John almost married
> Count Nicholas Ludwig von Zinzendorf—leader of Moravians
> Peter Bohler—Moravian leader and friend
> George Whitefield—persuaded John to preach in the fields
> Mary Vazeille—widow whom John married
> Dorothy Downes—class leader
> Sarah Crosby, Mary Bosanquet, Hannah Harrison, Eliza Bennis—some of the women who engaged in preaching

Activity 3: "What Is the Location?"

Give the name or identification of a location to each person. Have persons find the match to their name/identification. Follow directions for Activity 2.

> Epworth—place of John Wesley's birth
> Charterhouse—exclusive London school that Wesley attended for six years

Christ Church—Oxford college from which Wesley graduated
Lincoln College—Oxford college where Wesley had a fellowship
Savannah, Georgia—place where Wesley served as a missionary
Aldersgate Street, London—where Wesley had a heartwarming
    experience
New Room, Bristol—first chapel of Wesley's societies
Foundry—an old cannon factory remodeled for a chapel
Wednesbury—where one of the worst riots against Methodists
    occurred
City Road Chapel, London—John Wesley's burial place

(NOTE: Items from Activities 2 and 3 can be combined into one. If the group is small, select the most important items; or give list of people or places to teams of two, then ask them to identify each using Chapter 1. Or place the answers at various locations around the room.)

Introducing the Study

Discuss the overall aims of the study, the general outline, and expectations of the group. Introduce the basic resources. Emphasize that **everyone needs a copy of the book**. Assignments from the text and Bible readings are basic for everyone. The Enrichment Opportunities will enhance learning related to the study. Share something about yourself and your background in relation to the study. Give time for questions or comments.

Learning Activities

1. Life of John Wesley: Timeline

The sequence of events in the life of John Wesley is important in order to understand his faith journey and the foundations of Methodism. Place on the wall an 8-foot-long sheet of shelf paper (or pieces of newsprint taped together). Make a heavy horizontal line through the middle of the paper, from end to end. Put "1700" at the beginning of the line to the left and "1795" at the end of the line. Mark every inch on the line to represent one year. Give members of the group information about the events in the life of John Wesley to be read as the date is placed on top of the Timeline by the study leader, a designated person, or the person reading the information. (Date can be written on the Timeline with a marker, or tape small papers with the dates and brief description of event at proper places.) You can expand on the suggestions given below with information from the book or from supplementary books in the bibliography.

1703:   John Wesley was born June 17.

1709:   Parsonage at Epworth burned; John Wesley was the last saved from the fire. (Read words to "Behold the Savior of Mankind" in *The United Methodist Hymnal*, 293.)

1714–
1720:   Attended London's Charterhouse School.

1721–
1724:   Attended Christ Church College of Oxford University. Lived on 28 pounds a year, giving away all he did not need for clothing and sustenance. Became proficient in reading Greek New Testament.

1725:   Began a diary in a red notebook that had belonged to his grandfather, a Puritan preacher. John used a shorthand code that helped him to write fast and keep his intimate writings hidden from others. The code was not accurately decoded until 1972. John was ordained a deacon and assisted his father in ministry at Epworth.

1726:   Elected to fellowship at Lincoln College, which gave him opportunity for further study, tutorial work, free room, dinners, and an annual stipend.

1728:   Ordained to the Anglican priesthood at Oxford.

1729:   Became leader of small group of Oxford students who met regularly for spiritual growth known as "The Holy Club," "Bible Moths," "Sacramentalists," and "The Methodists."

1735:   Enlisted with Charles to be a missionary in Georgia.

1737:   First experienced Love Feast among Moravians. Romance with Sophia Hopkey. (Read stanza 2 of "Jesu, Thy Boundless Love to Me" in *The United Methodist Hymnal*, 183, and notes following the hymn). Published *A Collection of Psalms and Hymns*, the first English hymnbook published in America. Left for England in December.

1738:   Attended prayer meeting at Aldersgate and had "heartwarming" experience (read quote, page 6 in the book).

1739:   Persuaded by George Whitefield to begin field preaching in Bristol. (Read from Journal on page 7 in book.)

1744:   Riots against Methodists in Wednesbury (page 10 in book).

1751:   Married Widow Mary Vazeille.

1781:   Death of his wife, Mary.

1788:   Death of Charles Wesley.

1791:   John Wesley died. Some of last words were: "The best of all is, God is with us."

2. The Eighteenth Century and the Twentieth Century

Using the material in the book (Chapter 1) and other information gleaned from background reading, share with the participants the eighteenth-century setting. Make a chart on a chalkboard or newsprint with two columns headed "Eighteenth Century" and "Twentieth Century." List four categories down the lefthand side: "Political, Economic, Social, Religious." As study leader, place information under the "Eighteenth Century" column in each of the four categories as you present the background information. For example: in the column headed "Eighteenth Century," beside the category "Political" put: "continuing political struggle between two major parties, conservative Tories and reformist Whigs."

In teams of two, discuss what should be placed in the "Twentieth Century" column for each of the four categories. After five minutes, ask the teams to share with the entire group and to write the information on the chart in the "Twentieth Century" column.

Assignments for Session 2

Basic Assignment: Read Chapter 2 and Ephesians 2:1-10.

• Ask each person to select a favorite Charles Wesley hymn and to be prepared to give the reason for the selection.

• Assign each person to a "class" of five to seven members, and give each person a "ticket" for admission to his or her "class" at subsequent sessions. To identify each "class," place different colored borders around the "tickets." On the next page is an example of a "ticket," which can be copied or adapted for use. A 3-by-5-inch file card can be used.

"If you love me, keep my commandments."
(John 14:15)

Name _____

Date _____

Enrichment Opportunities: Ask group members to volunteer for activities to enrich themselves and the entire group. Volunteers should write their names beside the Enrichment Opportunity selected on the list that has been posted.

Closing Worship

Hymn: "I'll Praise My Maker While I've Breath" (verses 1 and 4, *The United Methodist Hymnal,* 60)

Prayer:
"Almighty God, in a time of great need
you raised up your servants John and Charles Wesley,
and by your Spirit inspired them to kindle a flame of sacred love
which leaped and ran, an inextinguishable blaze.
Grant that all those whose hearts have been warmed at these altar fires,
being continually refreshed by your grace, may be so devoted
to the increase of scriptural holiness throughout the land
that in this our time of great need,
your will may fully and effectively be done on earth as it is in heaven;
through Jesus Christ our Lord. Amen."
(*The United Methodist Book of Worship,* 439)

STUDY SESSION 2

Purpose: To explore Wesley's spiritual and theological concepts and their implications for today.

Objectives
- To examine the interrelation of Scripture, tradition, reason, and experience in Christian life;
- To consider major themes of Wesley's preaching and writings.

Preparing for the Session

- Display quotes from sermons and writings of John Wesley that are related to themes for the session:

  —"Plain truth for plain people."
  —"I am determined to be a Bible Christian, not almost but altogether."
  —"It is a fundamental principle with us that to renounce reason is to renounce religion, that religion and reason go hand in hand, and that all irrational religion is false religion."

- Make a poster with Wesley's instructions about studying Scripture:

  1. Read selected text
  2. Refer text to God in prayer
  3. Consult parallel texts
  4. Continually reflect and meditate
  5. Converse with knowledgeable people
  6. Examine other helpful writings
      (From "Preface" to John Wesley's *Forty-Four Sermons*)

- Materials needed for activities: Information about the events and persons for the Timeline; copies of the diagram of the Quadrilateral on page 153 for participants who do not have the book; a set of four different-colored circles and a paper fastener for each participant; a United Methodist hymnal for each participant.

Opening Worship

Moments of Reflection and Silent Prayer

Scripture: Ephesians 2:8, 9 (Reader 1, Scripture; Reader 2, *Explanatory Notes Upon the New Testament,* by John Wesley)

Reader 1: "For by grace ye are saved through faith;"

Reader 2: "Grace, without any respect to human worthiness, confers the glorious gift. Faith, with an empty hand, and without any pretence to personal desert, receives the heavenly blessing."

Reader 1: "And this is not of yourselves;"

Reader 2: "This refers to the fact that you are saved through faith."

Reader 1: "It is the gift of God: not by works, lest any man [person] should boast."

Reader 2: "Neither this faith nor this salvation is owing to any works you ever did, will, or can do."

Hymn: "Come, Holy Ghost, Our Hearts Inspire" (*The United Methodist Hymnal,* 603)

Prayer: "Concerning the Scriptures" (*The United Methodist Hymnal,* 602)

Class Meetings

The Methodist societies were divided into "classes" that met regularly. Wesley gave this description of a class:

> Many now happily experienced that Christian fellowship of which they had not so much as an idea before. They began to "bear one another's burdens," and naturally to "care for each other." As they had daily a more intimate acquaintance with, so they had a more endeared affection for, each other. And "speaking the truth in love, they grew up into Him in all things, who is the Head, even Christ."

Appoint a leader for each class (Wesley appointed men and women). Ask "classes" [persons with the same color ticket] to meet for twenty minutes to discuss: What would it mean to live/witness as if you have faith when you do not feel that you do? (Wesley did not feel assurance of faith. He asked his Moravian friend, Peter Bohler, whether he should stop preaching. Bohler told him to preach the kind of faith for which he was searching until he possessed it.)

In the total group have participants share responses.

Learning Activities

1. People and events during Wesley's Life: Timeline

Place "Age of Enlightenment" in the center above the Timeline. Give members of the class information about events and persons during the time Wesley lived. Follow the same procedure as in Study Session 1, except place the dates and brief descriptions below the Timeline.

1701:   *The Daily Courant,* the first daily newspaper, published.

1706:   Union of England and Scotland to create Great Britain.

1707:   Isaac Watts, Anglican bishop and hymn writer, published *Hymns and Spiritual Songs.*
        First practical steam engine built by Thomas Newcomen.

1712:   French philosopher Jean-Jacques Rousseau was born.

1714:   Death of Louis XIV, the "Sun King" of France.

1715:   Death of Queen Anne, last Stuart monarch, and accession of George I, the first Hanoverian king of England.

1721:   Parliamentary government began (with Prime Minister).

1742:   Handel's *Messiah* was first performed in Dublin.

1755:   Dr. Samuel Johnson published his Dictionary.

1776:   Declaration of Independence by American colonists.

1778:   Economist Adam Smith wrote *The Wealth of Nations.*

1780:   Robert Raikes opened his Sunday school in Gloucester.

1789:   Beginning of the French Revolution.
        Constitution of the United States of America ratified.

Note: This was the time of Voltaire, young Beethoven, Mozart, Hannah More, Madame de Pompadour, Mary Wollstonecraft Godwin, Daniel Defoe, Jonathan Swift, Sir Isaac Newton, Bonnie Prince Charlie, and Captain Cook. What other significant events or people can you think of?

2. Basis for Christian Decision-Making

  a. Ask the total group where the main themes of Wesley's theology can be found. List these sources on a chalkboard or newsprint.

  b. Introduce the diagram of the Wesleyan Quadrilateral on page 153. Discuss:
    (1) *Scripture*—as a primary source for Christian belief and faith (Refer to the poster with Wesley's instructions for studying Scripture.)
    (2) *Tradition*—as John Wesley understood it (Refer to the section on "Tradition" in the text.)
    (3) *Reason*—for analysis (Look at the quote about "irrational religion is false religion.")
    (4) *Experience*—as personal and corporate (Discuss the meaning of "inward experience" and "outward experience.")

  c. Give each person four different-colored circles and a paper fastener with the following instructions:
    (1) Write one of the four Quadrilateral words on each of the circles.
    (2) Arrange the circles so that the one with "Scripture" written on it is in the center with the edges of the other three underneath the center circle.
    (3) Put the fastener through the edges of the three and the center of the first circle. (Edges of the three circles will look like "petals" to the center circle.) All are linked together, but the one with "Scripture" remains central to the others

  d. Ask "classes" to discuss one of the following:
    (1) How have Scripture, Tradition, Reason, Experience helped you to make decisions?
    (2) Using the Quadrilateral, what should our response be to the poor?

3. Theology in Hymns

John Wesley referred to the first major Methodist hymnbook as "a little body of experimental and practical divinity." He used hymns from the early times of his ministry in Georgia. The hymns written by Charles Wesley were widely used by Methodists.

a. Ask each person to share a favorite hymn of Charles Wesley's and to give the reason for its selection. What message of the gospel is conveyed in each? List the hymns on newsprint or chalkboard. (See Index of Composers, etc., in *The United Methodist Hymnal*, page 922.)

b. Hymn Study: "Love Divine, All Loves Excelling" (*Hymnal*, 384) In groups of two or three ask participants to discuss the meaning of the words.

Assignments for Session 3

Basic Assignment: Read Chapter 3 and Ephesians 4:15-16.

● Instruct participants to look for the meanings of these mini-quotations found in Chapter 3:

(1) "means of grace"
(2) "grand means of drawing near to God"
(3) "extemporary"
(4) "Christian conference"
(5) "soaking"
(6) "works of piety"
(7) "works of mercy"

Closing Worship

Hymn: "Love Divine, All Loves Excelling" (*The United Methodist Hymnal*, 384)

Prayer: "O God, purify our hearts that we may entirely love Thee, and rejoice in being loved of Thee; that we may confide in Thee, and absolutely resign ourselves to Thee, and be filled with constant devotion toward Thee; that we may never sink into a base love of anything here below nor be oppressed with the cares of this life; but assist us to abhor that which is evil and cleave to that which is good. Give us true humility of spirit that we may not think of ourselves more highly than we ought to think. Keep us from being wise in our own conceits. Let our moderation be known to all. Amen." (John Wesley)

STUDY SESSION 3

Purpose: To reflect on the personal and communal means by which one can grow in the Christian faith.

Objectives
- To reflect on peaks and valleys of Christian life;
- To look at disciplines as part of spiritual growth;
- To consider ways to facilitate spiritual growth.

Preparing for the Session

- Materials needed for activities: information for the Timeline; copies of the checklist for "Works of Piety" for each participant; copies of the General Rules from the *Book of Discipline, 1996*, pages 70–72; "tickets"; water and crackers for the Love Feast.

- "Mini-Quotes" from Chapter 3 on a large sheet of paper or a chalkboard

- Post John Wesley's "General Rules for Employing Time":

  1. Begin and end every day with God; and sleep not immoderately;
  2. Be diligent in your calling;
  3. Employ all spare hours in religion; as able
  4. (Observe) All holy days;
  5. Avoid drunkards and busybodies;
  6. Avoid curiosity, and all useless employments and knowledge;
  7. Examine yourself every night;
  8. Never on any account pass a day without setting aside at least an hour for devotion;
  9. Avoid all manner of passion (John Wesley's *Diary*, 1725)

Opening Worship

Moments of Quiet and Reflection

Scripture: Ephesians 4:15-16 (Reader 1, Scripture; Reader 2, *Explanatory Notes Upon the New Testament,* by John Wesley)

Reader 1: "But speaking the truth in love, may grow up into him in all things, who is the head, even Christ";

Reader 2: "into His image and Spirit, and into a full union with Him";

Reader 1: "from whom the whole body fitly joined together . . . ";

Reader 2: ". . . all the parts being fitted for and adapted to each other, and most exactly harmonizing with the whole;

Reader 1: "And compacted by that which every joint supplieth . . . ";

Reader 2:". . . knit and cemented together with the utmost firmness . . . ";

Reader 1: ". . . according to the effectual working in the measure of every member, maketh an increase of the body to the edifying of itself in love";

Reader 2: "According as every member in its measure effectually works for the support and growth of the whole. A beautiful allusion to the human body, composed of different joints and members knit together by various ligaments, and furnished with vessels of communication from the head to every part."

Hymn: "Jesus, United by Thy Grace" (*The United Methodist Hymnal,* 561)

Prayer: "We depend upon Thee, especially for the grace of Thy Holy Spirit. May we feel it perpetually bearing us up, by the strength of our most holy faith, above all the temptations that may at any time assault us. Amen." (John Wesley)

Class Meetings

Ask participants to talk about the peaks and valleys in their Christian life and to share as appropriate with the entire group.

Learning Activities

1. Beginning of Methodist Societies: Timeline

John Wesley established a basic structure of Societies, a mark of Methodism for over a hundred years. The Methodist Societies were different from other religious societies because John Wesley directly supervised them. In "A Plain Account of the People Called Methodists," a letter that he wrote in 1748, Wesley tells of people wanting to meet with him regularly. He asked them to gather every Thursday evening, and he would spend time with them.

> They therefore united themselves "in order to pray together, to receive the word of exhortation, and to watch over one another in love, that they might help each other to work out their salvation."

1739:   Methodist Societies were begun in London and Bristol. Members of the Societies were divided into smaller groups known as "classes" or "bands" for spiritual conversation and guidance. A chapel, called New Room, was constructed in Bristol. In London, the Foundry, an old cannon factory, was purchased and renovated for a chapel, lodging for Wesley, and facilities for publishing and social ministry.

1742:   Organizing of first Methodist class meeting in Bristol.

1743:   Wesley codified examination process—The Nature, Design, and General Rules of the United Societies.

1744:   First Annual Conference was held in London to discuss theology, the mission of Methodism, and appointment of preachers to locations for the ensuing year.

1754:   Wesley began to write *Explanatory Notes Upon the New Testament* for "plain, unlettered" people.

1755:   Wesley wrote the Covenant Renewal Service.

1772:   Wesley published *Prayers for Children.*

2. Checklist for "Works of Piety"

Share with the total group the significance of spiritual disciplines in the life and teachings of John Wesley. Give an opportunity for participants to share thoughts about Christian disciplines.

Give each person a copy of the checklist below. Instruct all participants to place a check mark beside the Works of Piety that are part of their lives. Allow time for completion.

Checklist

__Read Bible daily __Use plan of study for Bible
__Pray daily (__morning, __evening, __mealtime, __other)
__Fast (__one day a week, __one meal a week, __other times)
__Participate in sacrament of Holy Communion
       (__regularly __infrequently)
__Attend corporate worship services regularly
__Participate in prayer, study, or support group
__Keep a journal
__Read other spiritual resources

Post an enlarged copy of the checklist at an appropriate place; ask group members to indicate their responses by placing a mark beside those they marked on their own checklists. This will give a profile of the group. (This can be done during break time or after the session.) Hold a discussion about the impact of pressures of life on time for faith development.

3. Definitions of the "Mini-Quotes"

Ask persons to share responses from their readings with the full group and to write the definitions beside the Mini-Quotes.

4. General Rules for Christian Living

Give each person a copy of the General Rules found in the *Book of Discipline, 1996* on pages 70–72. Return to class meeting groups to look at the General Rules and then develop "Rules for Christian Living Today" related to Works of Piety. Put them on a large sheet of paper.

Ask a member from each class to share the Rules that the class developed. Look for similarities.

5. Visit by Sarah Crosby

The class member who took the Enrichment Opportunity related to Sarah Crosby may use the following narration to tell her story. As study leader, introduce her as Methodism's first woman preacher.

> Shortly after my conversion in 1749, I had a burning desire to tell others about the love, joy, and peace that I had found in Christ. I joined the Foundry Society in October, 1750. Shortly after becoming a class leader in 1751, I had a vision of Jesus while I was praying. Jesus said, "Feed my sheep."
>
> I became involved with other women working among the poor and needy in London. This increased my desire to be instrumental in bringing people to God. In 1761, at a class meeting, I was so overwhelmed by the presence of the Lord and love for the people that I began to tell them about what the Lord had done for me. This was close to preaching, and John Wesley did not allow women to preach.
>
> I wrote to Mr. Wesley and told him what had happened and asked his authorization. He told me to testify about my religious experience and to read to the congregation and comment on one of his sermons or a passage from his New Testament *Notes.*
>
> Large audiences gathered as I traveled from place to place. In 1769, Mr. Wesley permitted me to exhort the congregation but told me never to take a text and not to speak longer than four or five minutes without a break. Finally, in 1771, Mr. Wesley advised me to use a Scripture passage as the basis for my "speaking."
>
> Mary Bosanquet wrote to Mr. Wesley and argued that, on the basis of her examination of Scripture, women were called sometimes by God to preach in extraordinary situations. Mr. Wesley did say that God has given certain women an "extraordinary call" to speak in public. He refers to this in his *Notes* on 1 Corinthians 14:34: "Let your women be silent in the churches— *Unless they are under an extraordinary impulse of the Spirit."* Mr. Wesley called this "speaking" instead of "preaching," but I don't think the people knew the difference.
>
> (Paraphrased from *She Offered Them Christ,* by Paul Chilcote. See the Selected Bibliography, page 155.)

Assignments for Session 4

Basic Assignment: Read Chapter 4 and 1 Corinthians 13.

- Interview three people about "Works of Mercy" in which the church is, or should be, involved today.
- Find the meaning of "Mini-Quotes" found in Chapter 4:
  (1) "grand pest of Christianity"
  (2) "snare of the devil"
  (3) "wholesomest" beverage
  (4) "liquid fire"
  (5) "execrable sum of all villainies"

Closing Worship: A Love Feast
(See *The United Methodist Book of Worship*, page 581.)

Work with the person(s) who accepted this as an Enrichment Opportunity to make it a meaningful experience. The ticket form below may be reproduced and used for the Love Feast. Each participant should be given a ticket to be collected by a person designated as a steward at the Love Feast.

Date _____

ADMIT THE BEARER TO THE LOVE FEAST

Name _____

"I give you a new commandment: Love one another; as I have loved you. . . . "

Additional Background Information: The first Methodist Love Feast was probably held by women, members of the Society of Bristol, on April 15, 1739. Love Feasts were usually held in the evenings, sometimes lasting from 7 P.M. until 10 P.M. Wesley said in his *Journal*: "Many were surprised when I told them, 'The very design of the love Feast is free and familiary conversation in which every man, yes, every woman has liberty to speak."

The early societies were often ridiculed because of their participation in the "Love Feast"—a term that outsiders did not understand. Admittance by ticket kept troublemakers out.

The story is told that on the Grimsby circuit in the 1750's, John Wesley himself was refused admission by the steward to the Love Feast, because he could not produce a ticket. Wesley heartily commended the steward to the people gathered for the Love Feast.

JOHN WESLEY

STUDY SESSION 4

Purpose: To consider how faithful discipleship and ministry are expressed through "Works of Mercy."

Objectives
- To become familiar with Wesley's view and "Works of Mercy" related to social issues of his time;
- To examine the statements and positions of The United Methodist Church with regard to social issues;
- To review historic involvements of women in "Works of Mercy," and to consider present and future actions.

Preparing for the Session

- Materials needed for activities: Information for the Timeline; copies of the Social Principles from the *Book of Discipline, 1996* for each participant; copies of the closing litany for each participant.

- Quotes:

   —"An ounce of love is worth a pound of knowledge."
   —"Be never unemployed; be never triflingly employed."
   —"The Gospel of Christ knows no religion but social; no holiness but social holiness."
   —"Do all the good you can;
   By all the means you can;
      In all the places you can;
   At all the times you can;
      To all the people you can;
   As long as ever you can."

- Provide a large piece of paper or space on a chalkboard for group members to write the results of their interviews. As people arrive, ask them to list the "Works of Mercy" in which the church is, or should be, involved.

Instead of repeating the same one, place a mark beside it each time it is mentioned.

● Add Mini-Quotes from Chapter 4 to the list from Chapter 3.

Opening Worship

Moments of Reflection and Silent Prayer

Scripture: 1 Corinthians 13:13 (Reader 1, Scripture; Reader 2, *Explanatory Notes Upon the New Testament,* by John Wesley)

Reader 1:   "And now abide these three, faith, hope, love; but the greatest of these is love."

Reader 2:   "Faith, hope, love are the sum of perfection on earth; love alone is the sum of perfection in heaven."

Hymn: "A Charge to Keep I Have" (*The United Methodist Hymnal,* 413)

Prayer: "Let thy unwearied and tender love to me make my love unwearied and tender to my neighbor, zealous to pray for, and to procure and promote his health and safety, ease and happiness; and active to comfort, succour and relieve all whom Thy love and their own necessities recommend to my charity. Make me peaceable and reconcilable, easy to forgive, and glad to return good for evil. Make me like Thyself, all kindness and benignity, all goodness and gentleness, all meekness and long-suffering. Amen." (John Wesley)

Class Meetings

Read the quotation from John Wesley about the essence of Christianity (page 57). Share personal involvement(s) in "outward holiness" or "social holiness." Are there other needs to which you should be responding? Share responses with the entire group.

Learning Activities

1. Reports From the Interviews

Give an opportunity for the group to share some of their experiences and observations from the interviews.

2. Wesley's Involvements in Social Holiness: Timeline

Follow the same procedure as in the other sessions.

1730:	Wesley preached once a month at two prisons.
1731:	Wesley started a small school for poor children with a woman to teach.
1746:	Small business loan program was begun.
1747:	Published *Primitive Physick, or An Easy and Natural Method of Curing Most Diseases.*
1748:	New Kingswood School was built outside Bristol.
1749:	Began to publish the Christian Library that finally contained fifty volumes.
1769:	Hannah Ball of Wycombe opened a Sunday school for training children in Scripture.
1778:	Published *Arminian Magazine* monthly (against predestinarianism).
Winter of 1783–84:	Spent five consecutive days walking the streets of London, which were ankle deep in mud, to raise about $1,000 in order "to clothe them that needed it most."
1787:	Wrote to Asbury deploring the genocide of Native Americans and urging renewed work among them.
1791:	Wrote last letter to William Wilberforce urging him to "go on, in the name of God and in the power of his might, till even American slavery, the vilest that ever saw the sun, shall vanish before it."

3. Interviews With Three Workers of Mercy

An interviewer and three women will be needed. The following information can be supplemented with material from books such as *She Offered Them Christ,* by Paul W. Chilcote (see Selected Bibliography, page 155).

After the interviews, ask the group members to share the names and involvements of other persons in early Methodism.

   a. **Grace Murray:** A member of the Foundry Society in London and a model leader in the early Methodist movement. In her memoirs she wrote:

   Mr. Wesley made me a Leader of a Band; I was afraid of undertaking it, yet durst not refuse, lest I should offend God. I was also appointed to be one of the Visitors of the Sick which was my pleasant work.

   John Wesley said: "May not women as well as men, bear a part in this honorable service? Undoubtedly they may; nay, they ought; it is meet, right and their bounden duty. Herein there is no difference, 'there is neither male nor female in Christ Jesus.' "

   After the death of her husband, Grace returned to northern England and was appointed one of the first class leaders of the newly established Society at Newcastle. She traveled through the northern counties of England and into Ireland to meet with the female societies. Wesley commended her work by saying: "I saw the work of God prosper in her hands. She was to me both a servant and friend, as well as a fellow-laborer in the Gospel."

   b. **Mary Bosanquet:** Mary was from a wealthy family. At an early age she was introduced to Methodism by a servant girl and became involved in a Society. She took seriously the preaching of Wesley about "give all you can" and used her resources to provide for the needy. She was appointed by Wesley to be housekeeper at Kingswood School in 1757 and proved to be an able administrator. With the assistance of Sarah Ryan, one born of poor parents, she took charge of a large house in Leytonstone in 1763 and opened it as a sanctuary for the most destitute and friendless in London. For over five years they gave shelter and care to thirty-five children and thirty-four adults. What could have been an elegant home was a school, an orphanage, a hospital, and a halfway house for some of the poorest.

   c. **Sarah Peters:** Use material from pages 63–64 in the study book.

4. Social Principles and "Works of Mercy"

Give each person a copy of the Social Principles. Ask those who volunteered for this Enrichment Opportunity to share their findings with the group. Give the other group members an opportunity to share their thoughts and observations.

Assignments for Session 5

Basic Assignment: Read Chapter 5 and Psalm 137.

Closing Worship

Hymn: "Forth in Thy Name, O Lord" (*The United Methodist Hymnal*, 438)

All: Inasmuch as you do it to one of the least of these, you do it to me. (Adapted from Matthew 25:40)

Left: "Gain all you can, save all you can, give all you can."

Right: "In all this I have given you an example that by such work we must support the weak, remembering the words of the Lord Jesus, for he himself said, 'It is more blessed to give than to receive.' " (Acts 20:35)

Left: "Whenever you have opportunity, do all the good you can, particularly to your poor, sick neighbor." (*On Visiting the Sick*)

Right: "I was naked and you gave me clothing, I was sick and you took care of me, I was in prison and you visited me." (Matthew 28:36)

Left: "Better is honest poverty, than all the riches bought by the tears, and sweat and blood of our fellow creatures." (*Thoughts Upon Slavery*)

Right: "He has sent me to proclaim release to the captives . . . to let the oppressed go free." (Luke 4:18b)

Left: ". . . with God's assistance to train up children in every branch of useful learning."

Right: "Train children in the right way, and when old, they will not stray." (Proverbs 22:6)

Left: "[People] in general can never be [considered] to be reasonable creatures, till they know not war anymore." (*The Doctrine of Original Sin*)

Right: "He shall judge between the nations, and shall arbitrate for many peoples; they shall beat their swords into plowshares, and their spears into pruning hooks; nation shall not lift up sword against nation, neither shall they learn war any more." (Isaiah 2:4)

All: "Inasmuch as you do it to one of the least of these, you do it to me." (Adapted from Matthew 25:40)

STUDY SESSION 5

Purpose: To present the development of The United Methodist Church with its strong emphasis on mission.

Objectives
- To learn about the development of Methodism and its leaders in North America;
- To emphasize the centrality in Methodism of mission and ministry to the whole person;
- To consider the major contributions of women in mission.

Preparing for the Session

- Materials needed for activities: information for the Timeline; large map of the world; copies of the PURPOSE of United Methodist Women for all participants (see below); eight pieces of different-colored yarn, each about three feet long; and two, foot-long pieces of string or two rubber bands.

Opening Worship

Moments of Reflection and Silent Prayer

Scripture: Psalm 137:4; Mark 16:15 (Reader 2 reads Scripture from Mark; Reader 1 reads Psalm 137:4 and from *Explanatory Notes Upon the New Testament,* by John Wesley)

Reader 1: "How could we sing the Lord's song in a foreign land?"

Reader 2: "Go ye into all the world, and preach the gospel to every creature."

Reader 1: "Our Lord speaks without any limitation or restriction. If, therefore, every creature in every age hath not heard it, either those who should have preached, or those who should have heard it, or both, made void the counsel of God herein."

Hymn: "A Charge to Keep I Have" (*The United Methodist Hymnal*, 413)

Prayer: "Send forth Thy light and Thy truth into all the dark corners of the earth, that all kings may fall down before Thee, and all nations do Thee service. Bless these kingdoms, and give us grace at length to bring forth fruits meet for repentance. . . . Prosper the endeavors of all who faithfully feed Thy people, and increase the number of them that the seed which hath been sown this day may take deep root in all our hearts; that, being not forgetful hearers but doers of the word, we may be blessed in our deeds. Amen." (John Wesley)

Class Meetings

Discuss: How have you sung the Lord's Song in a different, difficult setting? Share as appropriate with the entire group.

Learning Activities

1. Spreading the Word: Timeline

During John Wesley's ministry he traveled extensively, covering more than 250,000 miles on horseback in England, Wales, and Ireland. He preached more than 40,000 sermons. In addition, he was responsible for recruiting and sending many people to be in ministry in England, Ireland, and America. He believed that the news of the gospel was for all people. At the time of his death, there were 79,000 followers of Wesley's teachings in Britain and 40,000 in North America.

1735: While in Georgia as a missionary, Wesley met with Tomo Chachi, chief of the Creek Indians in Georgia.
1736: Wesley taught himself Spanish in order to communicate with Native Americans in Georgia who had been taught by Spanish Catholic missionaries.

1738: Wesley taught himself German in order to communicate with Peter Bohler and the Moravians.

1739: Wesley went to Wales for a five-day preaching tour.

1747: Methodism spread into Ireland with a new Methodist society started in Dublin.

1758: John Wesley baptized two "Negro slaves," at least one a woman, establishing a pattern for receiving people of color into the societies and the church. The two who were baptized returned to Antigua to start the Methodist society in the New World.

1769: Wesley sent two lay preachers, Richard Boardman and Joseph Pilmore, to America.

1771: Wesley sent Richard Wright and Francis Asbury to America.

1784: Assisted by two other Anglican priests, Wesley ordained two lay preachers for Methodist work in America and sent them with Thomas Coke to America. The Methodist Episcopal Church was founded at the Christmas Conference at Lovely Lane Chapel in Baltimore, Maryland.

2. Parade of "Saints"

Many people were involved in establishing Methodism in North America. Settlers from Ireland and England established societies patterned after those in which they had participated. Others were sent by Wesley on request from people in the colonies. Names of these persons and information about what they did are in Chapter 5. You can add to the names and information from other sources. (For example: Anne Schweitzer was an African American woman who became a founding member of the first Methodist society in Maryland.)

Option 1: Have participants who accepted this as an Enrichment Opportunity form a line and one by one share the names and information about contributions that persons made to the growth of Methodism in North America.

Option 2: Have participants who accepted this as an Enrichment Opportunity give only the information about the persons, and have other participants identify by name those described. This can be done individually by writing responses on paper, by giving an opportunity for anyone to give the identification following the description, or by forming teams of two or three participants to work on responses.

3. Mission Outreach

Reaching out to others with the gospel message continued in all the denominations that eventually formed The United Methodist Church. This outreach continues today.

Option 1: Place a large world map where it can be seen by the group.

Place these dates on the map: when mission work was begun in Africa, South America, and Asia; the beginning of the women's mission organizations in predecessor denominations; and the authorization of the office of deaconess in The Methodist Episcopal Church (see page 90). Give participants time to look at the map. Ask for their comments and observations about the areas where The United Methodist Church is in mission.

John Wesley believed in ministry to the whole person. Ask the group to discuss various kinds of mission ministries at the time of Wesley and today. How are they similar? How do they differ?

Option 2: Women have been major participants in the work of the church since the time of John Wesley. Today, United Methodist Women is the women's mission organization involved particularly with ministries with women, children, and youth.

Give a copy of the PURPOSE of United Methodist Women to each participant:

> The organized unit of United Methodist Women shall be a community of women whose PURPOSE is to know God and to experience freedom as whole persons through Jesus Christ; to develop a creative, supportive fellowship; and to expand concepts of mission through participation in the global ministries of the church.

In groups of three, ask them to discuss: What is the meaning of "participation in the global ministries of the church"?

4. Toward Union: From Many Into One

Refer to information on page 78 of the text. Put up the chart THE UNITED METHODIST CHURCH: TIMELINE OF UNION. (See page 154 for chart, which may be enlarged on a copy machine.)

a. Have five group members come to the front. Give each a different-colored piece of yarn approximately three feet long. To three persons give signs: "Methodist Episcopal," "Methodist Episcopal South," and "Methodist Protestant." (These can be attached to yarn and be placed around their necks or made "sash" style.) Ask these three persons to plait their pieces of yarn and tie the ends together with string or a rubber band. To two other persons give signs: "United Brethren" and "Evangelical Association." Ask them to braid together their two pieces of yarn and tie the ends with string or a rubber band. Next, ask one person from each of these groups to take the plaited and entwined pieces and to entwine them and tie the ends together. Attach the final entwined piece beside the chart. It represents five streams of our denominational history that have come together.

b. A group member with the sign "HOPE" comes forward and speaks:

HOPE FOR THE FUTURE: The union is not complete. Early in the history of our church, there were other divisions. These occurred primarily because of racism. African American members of the church were forced to sit apart from whites for worship. Three denominations were formed by African Americans—African Methodist Episcopal Church, African Methodist Episcopal Zion Church, and Christian Methodist Episcopal Church.

I bring HOPE that we will continue to confront our racism and work for union of all denominations from our Wesleyan tradition. A beginning is being made through covenant relationships in Churches of Christ Uniting and conversations between representatives of the various Methodist churches.

(This person places three different-colored pieces of yarn on the side of the chart opposite the entwined piece.)

Assignments for Session 6

Basic Assignment: Read Chapter 6 and Romans 12:1-5.

• Mini-Quote from Chapter 6: "practical divinity"

• Reflect on your theological explorations. Our *Book of Discipline, 1996*

146

states: "Theology is our effort to reflect upon God's gracious action in our lives. . . . Our theological explorations seek to give expression to the mysterious reality of God's presence, peace, and power in the world" (page 72).

Closing Worship

Hymn: "Forth in Thy Name, O Lord" (*The United Methodist Hymnal,* 438)

Prayer: John Wesley urged people to use *"ex tempore"* prayers. Ask class members to offer extemporaneous prayers for the mission and missionaries of our church.

JOHN WESLEY

STUDY SESSION 6

Purpose: To look at specific ways in which persons can utilize the strengths of Wesleyan heritage and theology to renew the church's life and ministry.

Objectives
- To consider present challenges to theology in the church;
- To explore ways to deal with differences in theological understandings;
- To understand the connectional nature of United Methodism;
- To renew our commitment to holiness of heart and life.

Preparing for the Session

- Quotes:

  —". . . as to all opinions which do not strike at the root of Christianity, we [Methodists] 'think and let think.' "

  —". . . to reform the nation, particularly the Church; and to spread scriptural holiness over the land."

  —"In essentials, unity;
  In others, diversity;
  In *all* things, charity."

- Mini-Quote: "practical divinity" (theology)

- Materials needed for activities: information for the Timeline; copies of "The Present Challenge to Theology in the Church" from *The Book of Discipline, 1996* (pages 80–81) for each participant; copies of the Covenant Renewal Service for each person from *The United Methodist Book of Worship* (page 288).

Opening Worship

Moments of Reflection and Silent Prayer

Scripture: Romans 12:4-5 (Reader 1, Scripture; Reader 2, *Explanatory Notes Upon the New Testament*, by John Wesley)

> **Reader 1:** For as in one body we have many members, and all members have not the same office: So we, being many . . .

> **Reader 2:** . . . and all believers . . .

> **Reader 1:** . . . are one body in Christ, and every one members of each other . . .

> **Reader 2:** . . . closely connected together in Christ, and consequently ought to be helpful to each other.

Hymn: "Jesus, Lord, We Look to Thee" (verses 1–5, *The United Methodist Hymnal*, 562)

Prayer: O God, we pray that we may live in peace and charity with all the world, especially among ourselves, united into one family, patiently forbearing, freely forgiving, and readily assisting one another. We beseech Thee to hear us, O Lord. Amen.

(Adapted from a prayer by John Wesley)

Class Meetings

Give these instructions:

Take a few minutes to reflect on your faith journey and theological explorations. Think about the persons or events that had an impact on you in your explorations. Share with the members of your class.

After a reasonable length of time, ask the full group to assemble. Share from the classes as appropriate.

Learning Activities

1. First Conference: Timeline

1744: (Add) John Wesley held the first conference of his British Methodist preachers to consider: "1. What to teach; 2. How to teach; and 3. What to do. . . . " The third topic included how the Methodists planned to integrate their doctrine, discipline, and practice of the Christian faith.

2. Dealing With Differences

(Place two chairs in the center of the room and arrange the other chairs in circles around them.)

Wesley had strong convictions and argued them vigorously. However, he also knew that he could be mistaken in some opinions.

> Although every man necessarily believes that every particular opinion which he holds is true (for to believe any opinion is not true is the same thing as not to hold it) yet can no man be assured that all his own opinions taken together are true ("Catholic Spirit").

Refer to pages 94–98 in the text to consider how Wesley dealt with "differences of opinion." Discuss how he responded and how we can respond to them today.

Select an issue such as inclusive language, welfare, or military spending. Ask two people with differing opinions (if possible) to volunteer to have a conversation about the issue. Seat them in the chairs in the center of the room and let them begin their conversation. When another person wishes to participate, he or she goes to the center, taps one of the two on the shoulder, and takes that person's place. Allow time for several persons to be involved in the discussion.

3. Theological Inquiry

Give each participant a copy of "The Present Challenge to Theology in the Church," *The Book of Discipline, 1996,* pages 80–81. In class groups, discuss responses to ecology issues using Christian theology as a basis. Encourage sharing with the total group.

4. Connecting Links

The author of the book states that "connection" was a mark of identity in the Methodist movement. Societies, bands, and classes were the early "connection." On pages 99–100 in the book, the present United Methodist connection is given. Scriptures use various images for connecting, such as the vine and branches and the body with its various members.

In groups of three, think of some image to describe the connection of The United Methodist Church. Share it with the total group.

5. Personal Renewal and Growth

John Wesley gave a pattern for renewal and growth that included the inseparability of "works of piety" and "works of mercy." This is a unique contribution of the Methodist tradition and heritage. In the opening worship of the General Board of the National Council of Churches of Christ in the USA meeting in New Orleans, November 10, 1994, "Offerings of the Communions to Christian Unity" were given. Following is the Offering of The United Methodist Church:

> The uniqueness of United Methodism and its gift to the Church catholic
> is the unity of grace and good works:
> grace that surrounds us before our awareness of it;
> grace that pushes us to grow toward God's love;
> grace that unites a warm heart and social witness;
>
> a heart habitually filled with love of God and neighbor;
> a social witness grounded in spirituality;
> a passionate concern for changed lives united with
> a prophetic concern for a changed society.

Make time for each group member to reflect on learnings from the study and to consider what would be helpful for personal spiritual renewal and growth. Then ask each to take a piece of paper and make two columns: title one "Works of Piety" and the other one "Works of Mercy." List in each column those "works" in which he or she will be involved. Have each individual write a statement of intent and sign it. This is personal and will not be shared with the class.

Closing Worship: Covenant Renewal Service

Use the service in *The United Methodist Book of Worship,* page 288. Share background material on page 288 with the group. Review and adapt it as needed. Hand out a copy of the service to each person.

If time is limited, use only "Wesley's Covenant Service," pages 291–94.

THE QUADRILATERAL

SCRIPTURE
(The Bible)

We rely on the way of salvation given in the Bible.

We use the Bible as a touchstone to examine real or supposed revelation.

We take it as our authority in matters of faith and practice.

Within Scripture is tradition, reason, and experience.

Thus we need to study and interpret it carefully.

EXPERIENCE
(New Life in Christ)

The Holy Spirit uses Scripture and tradition to bring us to faith.

By God's grace we receive a personal experience of faith.

There are variations of Christian experience; none can be normative.

Thus ours is a "heart religion," but it is not dependent on "feelings."

Religion must be relevant to our lives.

TRADITION
(Church's doctrine, order, worship)

We inherit the ancient church as well as create new traditions.

We use the writings of Christians through the centuries.

Traditions must be critiqued in light of the gospel's mandate for justice.

Historic doctrinal standards provide a springboard for our faith today.

REASON
(Critical Thought)

Reason is the means for giving structure to our beliefs.

Reason helps us order the evidence of revelation and helps guard against poor interpretation of Scripture.

But reason cannot prove or disprove God.

Adapted from a diagram in Doctrinal Standards and Our Theological Task: The Book of Discipline of The United Methodist Church, Part II—Leader's Guide, by Kenneth L. Carder (Nashville: Graded Press, 1989), page 61. (Originally published in The Gospel According to Wesley, Discipleship Resources, P.O. Box 840, Nashville, TN 37202.)

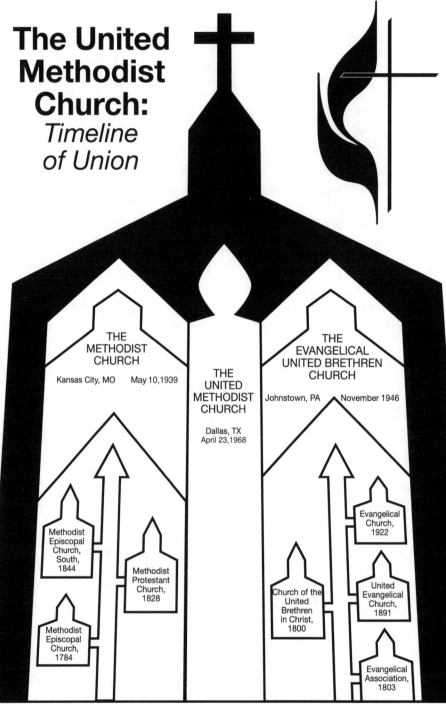

The United Methodist Church:
Timeline of Union

THE
METHODIST
CHURCH

Kansas City, MO   May 10, 1939

THE
UNITED
METHODIST
CHURCH

Dallas, TX
April 23, 1968

THE
EVANGELICAL
UNITED BRETHREN
CHURCH

Johnstown, PA   November 1946

Methodist
Episcopal
Church,
South,
1844

Methodist
Protestant
Church,
1828

Methodist
Episcopal
Church,
1784

Evangelical
Church,
1922

Church of the
United
Brethren
in Christ,
1800

United
Evangelical
Church,
1891

Evangelical
Association,
1803

Reprinted from the May–June 1992 issue of *New World Outlook,* copyright © 1992,
by permission of the editors.

SELECTED BIBLIOGRAPHY

Abraham, William J. *Waking From Doctrinal Amnesia: The Healing of Doctrine in The United Methodist Church*. Nashville: Abingdon Press, 1995.

The Book of Discipline of The United Methodist Church, 1996. Nashville: The United Methodist Publishing House, 1996.

The Book of Resolutions of The United Methodist Church, 1996. Nashville: The United Methodist Publishing House, 1996.

Chilcote, Paul W. *She Offered Them Christ: The Legacy of Women Preachers in Early Methodism*. Nashville: Abingdon Press, 1993.

Cobb, John B. *Grace and Responsibility: A Wesleyan Theology for Today*. Nashville: Abingdon Press, 1995.

Collins, Kenneth J. *The Scripture Way of Salvation: The Heart of John Wesley's Theology*. Nashville: Abingdon Press, 1997.

Dougherty, Mary Agnes. *My Calling to Fulfill: Deaconesses in the United Methodist Tradition*. New York: General Board of Global Ministries, 1997.

Gunter, N. Stephen, Scott J. Jones, Ted A. Campbell, Rebekah L. Miles, and Randy L. Maddox. *Wesley and the Quadrilateral: Renewing the Conversation*. Nashville: Abingdon Press, 1997.

Hampson, John. *Memoirs of the Late Rev. John Wesley*. London, 1791.

Heitzenrater, Richard P. *The Elusive Mr. Wesley: John Wesley His Own Biographer*. Nashville: Abingdon Press, 1984.

Heitzenrater, Richard P. *Wesley and the People Called Methodists*. Nashville: Abingdon Press, 1995.

Holifield, E. Brooks. *Health and Medicine in the Methodist Tradition*. New York: Crossroad, 1986.

Jennings, Theodore W., Jr. *Good News to the Poor: John Wesley's Evangelical Economics.* Nashville: Abingdon Press, 1990.

Jones, Scott J. *John Wesley's Conception and Use of Scripture.* Nashville: Abingdon Press, 1995.

Keller, Rosemary Skinner, editor. *Spirituality and Social Responsibility: Vocational Vision of Women in The United Methodist Tradition.* Nashville: Abingdon Press, 1993.

Keller, Rosemary Skinner, Hilah F. Thomas, and Louise L. Queen, editors. *Women in New Worlds: Historical Perspectives on the Wesleyan Tradition.* Nashville: Abingdon Press, 1981-1982.

Kimbrough, S T Jr. *A Song for the Poor: Hymns by Charles Wesley.* New York: General Board of Global Ministries, The United Methodist Church, 1993.

Langford, Thomas A. *God Made Known.* Nashville: Abingdon Press, 1992.

Maddox, Randy L. *Responsible Grace: John Wesley's Practical Theology.* Nashville: Abingdon Press, 1994.

Maddox, Randy, editor. *Rethinking Wesley's Theology for Contemporary Methodism.* Nashville: Abingdon Press, 1998.

Marquardt, Manfred. *John Wesley's Social Ethics: Praxis and Principles.* Nashville: Abingdon Press, 1992.

Maser, Frederick E. *The Story of John Wesley's Sisters, or Seven Sisters in Search of Love.* Rutland, VT: Academy Books, 1988.

Matthaei, Sondra Higgins. *The God We Worship.* Nashville: Abingdon Press, 1993.

McEllhenney, John G., editor. *United Methodism in America: A Compact History.* Nashville: Abingdon Press, 1992.

Oden, Thomas C. *John Wesley's Scriptural Christianity: A Plain Exposition of His Teaching on Christian Doctrine.* Grand Rapids, MI: Zondervan Publishing House, 1994.

Outler, Albert C., editor. *John Wesley. The Library of Protestant Thought.* New York: Oxford University Press, 1964.

Outler, Albert C. *Theology in the Wesleyan Spirit.* Nashville: Discipleship Resources, 1975.

Outler, Albert C. and Richard P. Heitzenrater, editors. *John Wesley's Sermons: An Anthology.* Nashville: Abingdon Press, 1991.

Runyon, Theodore. *The New Creation: John Wesley's Theology Today.* Nashville: Abingdon Press, 1998.

Thomas, James S. *Methodism's Racial Dilemma: The Story of the Central Jurisdiction.* Nashville: Abingdon Press, 1992.

Thorsen, Donald A. D. *The Wesleyan Quadrilateral: Scripture, Tradition, Reason, and Experience as a Model of Evangelical Theology.* Grand Rapids, MI: Zondervan Publishing House, 1990.

The United Methodist Book of Worship. Nashville: The United Methodist Publishing House, 1992.

The United Methodist Hymnal. Nashville: The United Methodist Publishing House, 1989.

Watson, David Lowes. *The Early Methodist Class Meeting.* Nashville: Discipleship Resources, 1985.

Wesley, John. *Explanatory Notes on the New Testament.* Peabody, MA: Hendrickson, 1987.

Wesley, John. *The Works of John Wesley.* Nashville: Abingdon Press, 1984. Projected to be 35 volumes.

Wesley, John. *The Works of the Rev. John Wesley.* Edited by Thomas Jackson. 14 volumes. Grand Rapids, MI: Baker Book House, 1978.

Whaling, Frank, editor. *John and Charles Wesley: Selected Prayers, Hymns, Journal Notes, Letters, and Treatises.* Ramsey, NJ: Paulist Press, 1981.

Wogaman, Philip. *To Serve the Present Age: The Gifts and Promise of United Methodism.* Nashville: Abingdon Press, 1996.

Videos

Clayride. Available from Ecufilm, 810 Twelfth Avenue, South, Nashville, TN 37203.

The Preacher: John Wesley. Available from Vision Video, P.O. Box 540, Worcester, PA 19490.